BY CHARLES BUKOWSKI

The Days Run Away Like Wild Horses Over the Hills (19
Post Office (1971)
Mockingbird Wish Me Luck (1972)
South of No North (1973)
Burning in Water, Drowning in Flame: Selected Poems 1955–1973 (1974)
Factotum (1975)
Love Is a Dog from Hell: Poems 1974–1977 (1977)
Women (1978)
You Kissed Lilly (1978)
*Play the piano drunk Like a percussion Instrument Until the fingers begin to bleed
    a bit* (1979)
Shakespeare Never Did This (1979)
Dangling in the Tournefortia (1981)
Ham on Rye (1982)
Bring Me Your Love (1983)
Hot Water Music (1983)
There's No Business (1984)
War All the Time: Poems 1981–1984 (1984)
You Get So Alone At Times That It Just Makes Sense (1986)
The Movie: "Barfly" (1987)
The Roominghouse Madrigals: Early Selected Poems 1946–1966 (1988)
Hollywood (1989)
Septuagenarian Stew: Stories & Poems (1990)
The Last Night of the Earth Poems (1992)
Screams from the Balcony: Selected Letters 1960–1970 (Volume 1) (1993)
Pulp (1994)
Living on Luck: Selected Letters 1960s–1970s (Volume 2) (1995)
Betting on the Muse: Poems & Stories (1996)
Bone Palace Ballet: New Poems (1997)
The Captain Is Out to Lunch and the Sailors Have Taken Over the Ship (1998)
Reach for the Sun: Selected Letters 1978–1994 (Volume 3) (1999)
What Matters Most Is How Well You Walk Through the Fire: New Poems (1999)
Open All Night: New Poems (2000)
*Beerspit Night and Cursing: The Correspondence of Charles Bukowski &
    Sheri Martinelli* (2001)
The Night Torn Mad with Footsteps: New Poems (2001)
Sifting Through the Madness for the Word, the Line, the Way: New Poems (2002)

CHARLES BUKOWSKI

the night torn mad with footsteps

NEW POEMS

ecco

An Imprint of HarperCollinsPublishers

HarperCollins books may be purchased for educational, business, or sales promotional use. For information, please e-mail the Special Markets Department at SPsales @harpercollins.com.

ACKNOWLEDGMENTS

These poems, written between 1970 and 1990, are part of an archive that Charles Bukowski left to be published after his death. On behalf of the author, the publisher would like to thank the editors of the periodicals where some of these poems first appeared.

Cover photo by Stephen Gottschalk.

First Ecco edition 2003.

Library of Congress Cataloging-in-Publication Data

ISBN 1-57423-165-0 (PAPER EDITION)
ISBN 1-57423-166-9 (TRADE CLOTH EDITION)

HB 08.22.2023

table of contents

1.

the
night
torn
mad
with
footsteps

1

like the fox
I run with the hunted
and if I'm not
the happiest man
on earth
I'm surely the
luckiest man
alive.

one writer's funeral

there was a rock-and-mud slide
on the Pacific Coast Highway and we had to take a
detour and they directed us up into the Malibu hills
and traffic was slow and it was hot, and then
we were lost.
but I spotted a hearse and said, "there's the
hearse, we'll follow it," and my woman said
"that's not the hearse," and I said, "yes, that's the
hearse."

the hearse took a left and I followed
it as it went up
a narrow dirt road and then pulled over and I
thought, "he's lost too." there was a truck and a man
selling strawberries parked there
and I pulled over
and asked
where the church was and he gave me directions and
my woman told the strawberry man, "we'll buy some
strawberries on the way back." then I swung
onto the road and the hearse started up again
and we continued to drive along
until we reached that
church.

we were going
to the funeral of a great man
but
the crowd was very sparse: the
family, a couple of old screenwriter friends,
two or three others. we
spoke to the family and to the wife of the deceased
and then we went in and the service began and the
priest wasn't so good but one of the great man's
sons gave a fine eulogy, and then it was over

and we were outside again, in our car,
following the hearse again, back down the steep
road
passing the strawberry truck again and my
woman said, "let's not stop for strawberries,"
and as we continued to the graveyard, I thought,
Fante, you were one of the best writers ever
and this is one sad day.
finally we were at the graveside, the priest
said a few words and then it was over.
I walked up to the widow who sat very pale and
beautiful and quite alone on a folding metal chair.
"Hank," she said, "it's hard," and I tried in vain
to say something that might comfort her.

we walked away then, leaving her there, and
I felt terrible.

I got a friend to drive my girlfriend back to
town while I drove to the racetrack, made it
just in time for the first race, got my bet
down as the mutuel clerk looked at me in wonder and
said, "Jesus Christ, how come you're wearing a
necktie?"

beagle

do not bother the beagle lying there
away from grass and flowers and paths,
dreaming dogdreams, or perhaps dreaming
nothing, as men do awake;
yes, leave him be, in that simple juxtaposition,
out of the maelstrom, lucifugous as a bat,
searching bat-inward
for a state of grace.

it's good. we'll not ransom our fate
or his for door knobs or rasps.
the east wind whirls the blinds,
our beagle snuffles in his sleep as
outside, outside,
hedges break, the night torn mad
with footsteps.

our beagle spreads a paw,
the lamp burns warm
bathed in the life of his
size.

a smile to remember

we had goldfish and they circled around and around
in the bowl on the table near the heavy drapes
covering the picture window and
my mother, always smiling, wanting us all
to be happy, told me, "be happy, Henry!"
and she was right: it's better to be happy if you
can
but my father continued to beat her and me several times a week
        while
raging inside his 6-foot-two frame because he couldn't
understand what was attacking him from within.

my mother, poor fish,
wanting to be happy, beaten two or three times a
week, telling me to be happy: "Henry, *smile!*
why don't you ever *smile?*"

and then she would smile, to show me how, and it was the
saddest smile I ever saw.

one day the goldfish died, all five of them,
they floated on the water, on their sides, their
eyes still open,
and when my father got home he threw them to the cat
there on the kitchen floor and we watched as my mother
smiled.

where was Jane?

one of the first actors to play Tarzan was living at the
Motion Picture Home.
he'd been there for years waiting to die.
he spent much of his time
running in and out of the wards
into the cafeteria and out into the yard where he'd yell,
"ME TARZAN!"
he never spoke to anyone or said anything else, it was always just
"ME TARZAN!"
everybody liked him: the old actors, the retired directors,
the ancient script writers, the aged cameramen, the prop men,
        stunt men, the old
actresses, all of whom were also there
waiting to die; they enjoyed his verve,
his antics, he was harmless and he took them back to the time
        when they
were still in the business.

then the doctors in authority decided that Tarzan was possibly
        dangerous
and one day he was shipped off to a mental institution.
he vanished as suddenly as if he'd been eaten by a
lion.
and the other patients were outraged, they instituted legal
        proceedings
to have him returned at once but
it took some months.

when Tarzan returned he was changed.
he would not leave his room.
he just sat by the window as if he had
forgotten
his old role
and the other patients missed
his antics, his verve, and

they too felt somehow defeated and
diminished.
they complained about the change in Tarzan
doped and drugged in his room
and they knew he would soon die like that
and then he did
and then he was back in that other jungle
(to where we will all someday retire)
unleashing the joyful primal call they could no longer
hear.

there were some small notices in the
newspapers
and the paint continued to chip from the hospital
walls,
many plants died, there was an unfortunate
suicide,
a growing lack of trust and
hope, and
a pervasive sadness:
it wasn't so much Tarzan's death the others mourned,
it was the cold, willful attitude of the
young and powerful doctors
despite the wishes of the
helpless old.

and finally they knew the truth
while sitting in their rooms
that it wasn't only the attitude of the doctors
they had to fear,
and that as silly as all those Tarzan films had been,
and as much as they would miss their own lost
Tarzan,
that all that was much kinder than the final vigil
they would now have to sit and patiently endure
alone.

the fish with yellow eyes and green fins
leaps into the volcano

sometimes dogs
in the alley
play the violin better
than the privileged peacocks
who swim in butter.
I speak now of young
dogs in
old rooms of peeling wallpaper and
the bathroom down the hall—always with
somebody in there.

you should have seen that place in Philly, just 2 dollars a week,
she said, and it was up under the attic
roof.
just what I need, I thought, I can live here FOREVER and
KREE-ATE.

god
it was HOT that first afternoon in there trundled away from the
world in my artistic sanctuary (Lawrence had Taos) but my
Taos was so HOT I drank my way through it, thinking, I will write
    at
night.

but when night came I passed out.

and I was to find that mornings were the worst: sick, I would
be awakened at 5 a.m. by 20 or 30 pigeons walking on the
roof—making their terrible sounds:
"koo, koo, koo..."

and I'd go to the little window and look out and there they would
be strutting about, shitting little white dots, their dumb rubber
    necks

jerking.

but I still knew (despite my 2-bit cheap insanity)
that there was an awful lot of bad writing out there being
called great, which really was no better than what I could
do under that Philly roof

but I decided to get out of there
and find another place to live and write
and maybe some day give the haters something real to
hate.

1966 Volkswagen minivan

there goes Bach again but
one wonders how much longer we can hold on?
it's good music
great music
but I mean and I wonder:
how much longer will we be able to hear
what he has to say?
question marks are sometimes
discouraging.
as we become more and more
dispossessed
giants like Bach will vanish
from our thoughts and lives and
the taste and touch of his music
will be like finding my love dead
just dead
eyes closed
her body still soft
still warm
her hair spilling over my forearm.

I listen to Bach as often as I can
and my love is driving over here this evening
in her 1966 Volkswagen van
as I chill the wine and wait.

her hair is the strangest color:
red mixed with gold
as conquering armies
smash snails
smash daffodils.

she has small hands
small feet.

we fight
we often laugh.

I am listening to Bach now.
the music stops.

she drives that damned mini-bus like a
rowboat over the rapids

if she would listen to my heart
she'd go slower
much slower.

please let me die
first because
I am older
much older.

listen Bach, your god and my god
are real but
helpful only in spurts.
I want you to
tell me that everything is all
right
and that her red and gold hair will be
spread
upon my pillow again.

her small feet
her small hands
her fingers stroking my eyes and
my ears and her laugh comforting
me.

his cap

there was an old guy used to walk his
dog in the neighborhood;
the dog wasn't particularly interesting
and neither was he.
the dog was black-and-white, spotted,
medium-sized and
the old guy
wore baggy pants and a sweater, but
most appealing was the small cap which he
wore
flat on top of his head
almost like an afterthought.
I used to watch him walk his
hound
(they were both medium-sized)
just as evening was slipping into
night.
they gave the neighborhood a sense of
peace and predictability
and an old-school stability
that we needed.

they *made* the neighborhood.

the evening finally came when
the old guy and the dog
were walking along the sidewalk
toward me
as I walked toward them.

as they came closer I hesitated.
the hound was sniffing,
moving forward, jerking at the leash
and the old guy
followed

neither leading nor being
led
and since it was such a pleasant evening
I wasn't afraid to speak:

"hi there!" I said.

"good evening," he said.

the hound moved on past me
and the old guy followed him along.
he and the dog went off down
the street, the dog stopping
now and then to
examine the
lawns.

I watched them as they went
to the corner where they
made their turn and were
gone.

it was not long after that
that I moved out of the
neighborhood.

•

personally, I might stop
writing stuff like this someday
if I can find a way
short of death and/or
senility

but, personally, things like
that old guy, his cap and his spotted
dog make it hard
to stop.

luck from a kitchen

what matters is still being here in
this kitchen with my small radio, this
rolled cigarette and
with a two-foot stack of fresh blue
laundry.
I'm sure I've sprayed
the last of the roaches and
what matters is that this tabletop
is littered with new poems.
two drunks fight in the apartment
to the rear, the cats walk
up and down the courtyard
and around the corner
girls sit in massage parlor
doorways
dreaming of love.

what matters is that I still have
after all that has preceded
poems left
me left
and these walls that I have always
loved
in all the cities and in all the
places I have lived,
these walls are still here and
my radio plays.
this Royal Standard typer
(which I have had for 7 years)
sometimes doesn't work for 2 or
3 days and then my hair begins to
fall out, I have trouble
pronouncing a simple sentence,
I break out in an itchy
rash and then

the Royal begins again
almost by itself.
that matters much more than
those two drunks fighting in
the apartment to the rear
or the flame of heaven locked tight
inside my coffee jar.

my radio gives me good, kind
music tonight.

it was just a little while ago

almost dawn
blackbirds on the telephone wire
waiting
as I eat yesterday's
forgotten sandwich
at 6 a.m.
on a quiet Sunday morning.

one shoe in the corner
standing upright
the other laying on its
side.

yes, some lives were made to be
wasted.

the fight game

a new boy:
he runs off 7
straight wins and
they put him in with the
old tiger.
a 2-to-one
underdog
he gets a split decision win
over the
tiger.

then at even money
he knocks off the
#3
challenger.

now he's seen in the
nightspots
always a new girl on his
arm
and there are whispers of the
needle.

he's no longer angry in the
gym
and each new girl on his
arm
is sexier than the
last.

then it's in the papers:
he punches a cop who pulls him over
for speeding.
he gets in a fight
something about a guy who

cut him off in
traffic.

but he's bailed
out smiling and
confident.

then he signs to
meet the #2 challenger

and against #2
he has no punch
no speed
no footwork and
he's k.o.'d in the
3rd.

next they put him with a guy
from Philly
who hasn't fought in 3
years.

the guy gets him in
1:59 of the
first.

they put the guy from Philly in
with the old
tiger and

the old tiger gets him
in 1:33 of the
second.

and where do the sexy girls go?
from Rome to Hong Kong
where do they go?

they too go back
finally
to the semi-finals and

the 4-rounders.

it works that way
for almost everyone.
sorrow is not
always quick to arrive but
it's always
waiting
there.

a lady who wants to help?

Chinaski, she says, sitting in the chair across
from me
her dress pulled up
around her fat legs
the varicose veins peeking at me
like little blue snakes
her dirty garter belt tugging at stubborn
flesh
her full mouth heavy with lipstick like
an animal mouth in a dream gone bad
her breasts like water balloons gone
mad with sagging

Chinaski, she says, you think you
write great stuff but it's all only
a pisspot full of dirty
words!

then she leans back and lights a
cigarette
inhales
exhales a stinging cloud of vile smoke
at me and
then asks,
well?

I don't think you've ever really read my
stuff, I tell
her.

bullshit, she says, recrossing her
legs, now what I wanna suggest
is that we form a writing
partnership.
we'll work together

as a team
and publish everything
under your name.

you mean, I ask, that you'll clean up my stuff
make it respectable
move in here with me
and scratch my back with
yours?

exactly.

I think not, I tell
her.

well, fuck you then! she
screams.

thank god, I think,
as she storms out of the room
thank god you
never will.

Carson McCullers

she died of alcoholism
wrapped in a blanket
on a deck chair
on an ocean
steamer.

all her books of
terrified loneliness

all her books about
the cruelty
of loveless love

were all that was left
of her

as the strolling vacationer
discovered her body

notified the captain

and she was quickly dispatched
to somewhere else
on the ship

as everything
continued just
as
she had written it.

a happening

he was always a first-rate jock,
I've watched him ride for many years
on many an afternoon at Del Mar, Hollywood Park,
Santa Anita.

early this year
his wife committed a terrible
suicide.

those who knew him well said that
he would never ride
again.

and he didn't ride for a
while.

then one afternoon he
accepted a mount
and as the horses came out
for the post
parade
and he rode into
view
the applause
began—a gentle
steady applause—it
continued for many
minutes
and many a sentimental
horseplayer
had to
turn away
to hide the
tears.

then
in that race
he came driving
down the stretch
just to miss
at the photo finish.

all he said later to the
reporters was: "it seems to
strange to come home and
not find her
there."

since then
he has been riding
with a style and an
abandon that is
unbelievable:
driving through small gaps
between horses
or dangerously along the
rail.

he is now
the leading jock
and
he continues to
win.

people have not seen
such riding in
decades.

he's the tiger in the
sun.

he's each one of us
alone
forever
fiercely ignoring
the
pain.

albums

I sat in my cheap room, a young man
totally out of place in the world.
I hardly ate, just wine and
classical music
sustained
me.

I lived like a god-damned fly, or maybe like
a confused
rat.
where I scrounged funds, I no longer
remember.

but I do remember the record store
where you could exchange 3 used albums for
2.

by buying the occasional album and by continuously
trading
I gradually listened to almost all the
classical albums
in that store.

but since I was broke most of the time
I was often forced to play the 2 albums
on hand
over and over and
over.

I drank and listened
until
each note and musical phrase
on those albums
became part of
me

forever.

now
decades later
I sometimes hear
one of those familiar albums
on the radio—
the same conductor, the same
orchestra—
and I immediately
turn the volume
up

and fondly remember
that distant
melancholy
time.

makeover

it's not hard to tear up
a bad poem.
it's much harder to discard
a woman who was once
good
but has now been destroyed by
drugs
and has become something
harsh and
fragmented.

where did she go
and why?

it's not hard to tear up
a bad poem
you can probably write
a better one.

but when a human being is destroyed
is there always a reason?

of course, of course, of
course.

but the grief is just
the same
and the joke
is one of the dirtiest ones
in this town or
in any other town
where the dead deal
death
to the dying.

centuries of lies

an acquaintance writes from Paris
to say
that they are still
talking about the time
I fucked up
on French prime time
TV
some years ago.

it's all a laugh to me now
because I remember so very little
about it
but it manages to sell
a few extra copies of my books
over there
to some intellectuals
for all the wrong reasons.

it was the same with the critics
who thought it was great
that I didn't want to visit
Sartre.

the critics believed that I was putting
him
down
when it was only that
I didn't know what to say
to the old man
who I thought was a very fine
writer.

it seems that when things get
rolling your way
you get more and more credit

for accomplishing great things than you
never even thought of

and soon an extra layer of myth
surrounds your work
that is not to be believed
but it is believed
nonetheless
and that is why so many
so-called geniuses are really
assholes
and why so many assholes are
so-called literary
critics.

too tough to care

there's this great big guy who comes to see me, he sits
in my big chair and starts smoking his cigars
and I bring out the wine
and we pour it down.
the big guy just gulps them down and I gulp
right along with him.
he doesn't say much, he's a stoic.

other people say, "Jesus, Hank,
what do you see in that guy?"
and I say, "hey, he's my hero, every man has to have a
hero."

the big guy just keeps lighting cigars and drinking.
he never even gets up to piss, he doesn't have
to.
he doesn't bother.

he smokes ten cigars a night and matches me
drink for drink.
sometimes he drinks even more
than I do.
he doesn't blink.
I don't either.

even when we talk about women we
agree.

it's best when we're alone because he never
talks to other people.

somehow I never remember him
leaving.
in the morning the chair is still there

and all the cigar stubs and
all the empty bottles but he's
gone.

what I like best is that he never disturbs the
image I have of him.
he's a tough son-of-a-bitch and I'm a
tough son-of-a-bitch
and we meet about once
every 3 months and put on our little
performance.
anything more than that would
kill us
both.

funny man

Mr. Geomethel liked to give parties on Saturday afternoon
at his home. we always got an invitation. I think it was
my 3rd or 4th wife, she always wanted to go, and she'd
keep at me until it was more miserable to stay home with her
than to go there. so that day she won, we drove to Echo
Park, parked above on the hill, stared down at the small
grey house, the people standing in the yard looking as dull
as last week's race results. however, she seemed to be
excited to see them. I suppose I kept her too much away
from that sort of thing, she was a country girl, honest and
healthy and full of fondness for people and fun. (me, I
liked to eat candy bars in bed alone with just her as she had
the most marvelous dark brown eyes.) we went down the path
to where many people were standing in the sun with Mr.
Geomethel beside the little grey house with the many chuck
holes in the neglected lawn and everybody holding tight to
some odd impulse, some mysterious reason for being there (but
when you looked hard into their eyes you could see just a
shadow of doubt in the back of their brains). my country
girl liked everybody, not only Mr. Geomethel but Chuck and
Randy and Lila and Creasefoot (the dog). she, my 3rd or 4th
wife, went from this person to that, from this group to that,
finding intense and interesting things to discuss. I drank
what I could of the very bad wine. I vomited secretly behind
a bush as she suddenly vanished, wanting me to search for her,
puked again, drank a bit more, waited and said yes or
no to a few questions passing by in the air. then she
appeared once again to tell me that Mr. Geomethel had taken
her to his bedroom to show her his paintings, and she was
surprised, she said, because they were *very* good.

every man, I answered her, probably has some kind of talent
if you look long enough. Mr. G's talent, I continued, was
probably his *very* good paintings.

she seemed angry at that, showed me her back and walked up
to 2 young men leaning against a collapsing wood fence.
they seemed happy to see her.

I went inside to the kitchen, opened a cupboard and found
an almost full pint of vodka. I poured a ¾ vodka and
¼ water. I found a Pall Mall in the sink and lit it.
I knew that my 3rd or 4th marriage was over because
of my jealousy and envy and many other horrible things.
"you lack self-confidence," she often told me. I knew that
and I was glad that she knew that. I had a bit more of my
drink then went into the yard and when she sneaked a look
at me she knew that I had passed over to the other side and
that I would not be coming back to her because of all the
terrible things. I felt wonderful, like a mallard rising
from the marsh, with the hunters
too drunk in their boat to shoot me down for their dogs
to swim out and drag back.
still, she walked over and tried:

"well, I suppose you want to *go* now, just when things are
starting to be fun?"

I'd like to go, I said, but this party is as good as any.
I can stay.

for me? she asked.

for us, I said, as finally I was no longer bored
and when Mr. Geomethel came up and asked me how things
were going I told him that I liked his party.
"I thought you were a *recluse?*" he said.
I am, I told him.

now my wife #4 or #5, she doesn't like parties but, of
course, there are numerous other problems.
I still get these regular invitations to Mr. Geomethel's
parties.
I toss them away neither in hatred nor in joy
and wife #3 or #4 phones me sometimes,
weeps,

46

says that what she misses is my humor, it's such a rare
thing, and I wonder about that because I can never
remember her laughing
except with other people
or at Mr. Geomethel's parties.

a fan

Harry the Horse
used to write me from jail
and I'd write him back. he said that of all the writers he
had written only Ginsberg and I had written back. he
purchased my books and passed them around.
that jail like anyplace else was full of writers and critics
and like the rest most of them hated me. Harry the
Horse defended me. he told them that even though I couldn't
write a decent sentence I *had* done time.

Harry came to see me when he got out, he came with another
x-con who had gotten out a bit earlier. I was then living
at my girlfriend's place and they stood in front of the fire-
place looking at my girlfriend and mentally running their zippers
up and down. I never asked what they had gone in for but
that gave me an idea. they didn't stay long, they had their
old ladies with them and their old ladies wanted to see
Disneyland. they had jobs as carpenters and made more in 3
days than I made in a month. we shook hands and said goodbye.

I got a letter last week. Harry the Horse was back in. he
said it was a parole violation. I believed him.
a con once told me: "nobody's guilty in here."

Harry wants to know where he can get my latest book. he's
typing 12 hours a day in that cell. that's one thing about
prison: you don't get many interruptions. I suppose
Ginsberg will answer him again and I will too. I'd rather
have readers and friends in there than in Paris or heaven.
now what the hell did I do with his letter?

Christ in his manger

it was an Irish mother and daughter from
New Jersey.
they lived in back
and peeked from behind the curtains
and watched all the action in our apartment
building. the girl was 28 and the mother was
in her 50s.
they saw no men.
they walked the streets together at noon.
they were on relief of some kind.

then ownership of the apartment changed
hands
and they were made managers
at $2 a day.
it must have been the first job for
either of them.

they had my phone number.
my nights became more difficult.
the phone would ring:
"say, we hoid screamin' down there!
is somebody gettin' killed?"

"no, no, it's all right."

"we gotta have *quiet* in dis building!"

as the nights went on they called
the police several times.
the police would come to the door and I would
send them away.

the ladies had 2 cats which they
never let outside.

the cats would sit in the window
numbed and crazed while the
ladies watched daytime TV.

each morning I was awakened as
they dragged a large tin tub
down the walk.
they raked and swept and put the
leaves, papers and refuse into the tub
which they dragged along by a rope.
then they watered.

most nights I went to
bed about 3:00 a.m.
they began their operations at
7:00 a.m.

the girl used a nozzle with a
thin hard stream and she liked to
hose down the large banana leaves.
the sound was unbearable. she
believed she was washing away the plant
lice.

one memorable night the girl came over
and with
her mother standing behind her
she said:
"say, we hoid loud *laughter*! we can't
have loud *laughter* around here! it's
afta ten p.m.!"

the owners finally moved the ladies into
another building they owned half-a-block
away and the ladies managed both apartments
for the same $2 a day.
it was better for me with them down there.
I didn't have to hear them complain:
"de owners say you can't pick de flowers!"
"no shoppin' carts allowed on de property!"

50

or read their signs:
"brake up cartons before putting in trash!"
"do not step in gardens!"
"no parking! cars will be hauled away!"
"do not pick flowers!"
but best of all
the police calls stopped.

I had to walk half-a-block to
pay the rent.
one Jan. 15 they still had a
cardboard Christmas tree on display and
a cardboard fireplace with
cardboard logs
and a little cardboard
Christ in the manger.
the mother had bought the daughter
a 5-foot stuffed giraffe.
I stood and waited for the
rent receipt.
I got it and then the girl handed me
a soiled piece of paper.

"some people don't like us. couldja
sign this petition? it's fa' the
owners ..."

and in the girl's handwriting:
"I hereby agree that Lucy and Betty are
good managers and doing a good job and I
want them to stay."

I signed the paper. they thanked me and
I left.

there was a drought in the city
and it continued.
the city put restrictions upon cosmetic
watering.
the ladies didn't come down to sweep
and water any longer.

but they were busy with the other place
which was littered with bottles, rocks, all
manner of garbage and debris.
a wild bunch of
party-givers lived there.
they were mostly unable
to speak English and they
liked to listen to the music of their
native land at more than full
volume
so the ladies were kept busy.
meanwhile, I didn't have to stop typing at 10 p.m.
any longer.
I went on merrily typing my poems and
stories until 3 a.m.

but one night they were back. they
knocked on the door. there was the
girl with her mother standing behind
her.

"say, who planted dese
little plants out here?"

"my girlfriend planted those."

"well, de owners say
ya can't do that!"

"why not?"

"well, we have dese seeds and we're
gonna landscape in da spring!"

they had bought a few packets of seeds the
year before, stuck them in the ground, put up
little string fences but nothing had grown.

"you're going to landscape?"

I was in my Japanese robe and smoking a

mangalore ganesh beedie.
it was 7:30 p.m. and the first drink
was waiting and the first poem was in the
typer.

"yeah, we got seeds. we're waitin' until
spring. so de owners say meantime ya can't plant
nothin'."

"ladies, please tell the owners that I will
protect each plant until death. that is final."

they just looked at me.

"what kinda plants are dose?" the girl asked.

"hell, I really don't know."

they turned and side by side they
walked away together
in the moonlight.

it was rather cold for them to still be out on the
street. as I watched they came to a shopping
cart halfway down the block.
they pushed it off the sidewalk and
left it near the curb.
then they headed east
together
I presume
to attend to their other
responsibilities.

the priest

we saw the priest in the ice cream
store.
he saw us and he smiled and
said, "hi, boys!"
he was eating a double-decker vanilla cone
and he left while we were getting
ours.

we went outside to eat our
ice cream.
the priest was gone.
we talked as we ate.

"he's a nice guy."

"yeah, he spoke to us."

"he eats ice cream."

"he's a real guy!"

"I wish all the priests were
like him!"

"I'll bet he even goes to the
movies."

"sure, we've heard him talk
about them from the
pulpit."

"he doesn't like most of them."

"but he likes ice cream!"

"that's something."

"sure!"

we had finished our
cones.
we stood there.

"what'll we do
now?"

"let's go visit the
priest."

"naw!"

"o.k., then what?"

"anything..."
we finally decided to look for
returnable
bottles.

the priest was a nice
guy
but we didn't want to jinx
our
summer.

1810–1856

one day Robert Schumann threw himself into
the Rhine and was then committed to an asylum
for the remainder of his life.

his wife, Clara, angrily held back his musical
compositions and
refused to permit them to be played.

one might think that she was his greatest protector and
critic.

one might think many things,
I suppose,
but I'm glad I'm listening to Robert
instead of to Clara
tonight.

back to the machine gun

I awaken about noon and go out to get the mail
in my old torn bathrobe.
I'm hung over
hair down in my eyes
barefoot
gingerly walking on the small sharp rocks
in my path
still afraid of pain behind my four-day beard.

the young housewife next door shakes a rug
out of her window and sees me:
"hello, Hank!"

god damn! it's almost like being shot in the ass
with a .22.

"hello," I say
gathering up my Visa Card bill, my Pennysaver coupons,
a Dept. of Water and Power past-due notice,
a letter from the mortgage people
plus a demand from the Weed Abatement Department
giving me 30 days to clean up my act.

I mince back again over the small sharp rocks
thinking, maybe I'd better write something tonight,
they all seem
to be closing in.

there's only one way to handle those motherfuckers.

the night harness races will have to wait.

love dead like a crushed fly

in many ways
good times had finally arrived
even though
I was still living in a
bombed-out apartment just off the
avenue.

I had climbed my way up through
many layers of terrible
adversity.

being an uneducated man
with
wild mad dreams—finally
many of them had actually come
true (I mean, if
you're going to try
you might as well fight
for the whole enchilada).

but almost
at once
(as such things occur)
the lady I loved dearly
took off
and began to
fuck
around the clock
with
male and female
strangers
imbeciles
and (to be fair)
probably with some fairly

decent folk.

but
(as such things occur)
it was without
warning
and I was left with
a pitiful dull languor of
disbelief
and
a painful mindless
clawing at my
heart.

also
as the tide
turned
I broke out
with a huge boil
on my back
nearly the size of an
apricot, well, a
small apricot
but still a
monstrosity and a
horror.

I pulled the phone
from the wall
locked the door
pulled down the shades and
began to
drink
just to pass the time of
night, and I went
mad, probably,
but
in a new strange and
delicious
sense.

I found an old recording of
Careless Love
and played it
over and over—
the hopelessness
of that blues record
fitting exactly into my
cage
my place
my own
disenchanted mood:
love dead like a crushed
fly.

I reached back and
wandering through my recent
past, I realized that as a
human being
I could have been much
better, nicer, kinder,
not just to her
but also to
the grocery clerk
the corner paperboy
the uninvited visitor
the ragged beggar
the tired waitress
the stray cat
the sleepy bartender
and/or
etc.

we keep coming up
short again and
again
but then we think that
ultimately, perhaps,
we are not so terrible
after all, and then we
find ourselves with

a girlfriend who
fucks
around the clock
plus we get
a boil nearly the
size of a small
apricot.

ah, remorse!
ah, grief!

and that record of
Careless Love
played as loud as possible
over and over and over
again!

what a time it was
as I stumbled over the beer and
whiskey bottles
the discarded laundry
the unread newspapers
the regrets and
the memories
all scattered across the
room.

I finally came out of it
a week later only
to find her standing
in my doorway
on a 9 a.m. Sunday
morning

her hair neatly
done,
her face
carefully made up,
in a fresh dress,

smiling,
as if the slate
had been
wiped clean—

she stood there
just a
dumb
game-playing
bitch—

having tried the many
others and
finding them (in
one way or the
other)
insufficient

she was
back (she
hoped)
as I poured her a
beer and
tilted the Scotch
into my nearly empty
glass

all the while
hearing
in my mind
the never-to-be-forgotten
song about
Careless Love.

but if my love for her had
ended
something else was about to
begin

as she crossed her long
legs
flashed her radiant
smile
and said,
brightly, "well, what have you
been doing while I was
gone?"

it beats love

I like symphony music but the first thing on waking
she turns on the radio and we have nonstop Brahms or Ives
or Stravinsky or Mahler or Beethoven or Mozart. She slices
the grapefruit and boils the eggs, counting the seconds:
56, 57, 58. she peels the eggs, brings everything to me
in bed, including the coffee. we feel like we're man and wife.
after breakfast it's the couch, we put our feet on the same
table and listen to more classical music. now she's on her first
glass of scotch and her third cigarette. it's been two nights
and two days like this. I tell her I want to go to the track. "when
will I see you again?" I ask. she suggests that that might be up
to me. I suggest next Wednesday around one p.m. she
nods. I nod. we nod. Wagner plays.

the automobiles of DeLongpre

how dare I sleep from 5 to 7:30 p.m.
while probably somewhere
soldiers fight to the death for a mountain or a
road
and while in this very city
many housewives bend wearily over the supper dishes.

frankly, there isn't enough to understand or dramatize
in this life;
that's why great poets go sour
and the average poet remains a
bore. poets simply make up more
than there is.

the phone rings and somebody asks me
if I want to hear Ginsberg read
tomorrow.

no no, I say, Ginsberg's all right but—

would I like to hear Creeley read the next day?

no no, Creeley's all right but—

I go back to bed and listen to the cars
driving along DeLongpre. someday I'll write an epic
poem about listening to the cars on DeLongpre
from my bed at 7:25 p.m. will I be making up
more than there is? it's certainly a literary conceit,
those automobiles of
DeLongpre, and the wives, and those troops
taking a mountain.

death is not the problem; waiting around for it
is.

40 years ago

in our cheap hotel room near
the Union Station, at 3 a.m., Jane and I had been
drinking cheap wine since noon. I was walking barefoot back and
forth across the rug, picking up shards of broken glass
(in the daylight you could see them under the skin,
blue lumps working toward the heart). I felt powerful in
my torn shorts, ugly balls hanging out, my
worn undershirt spotted with cigarette burns.
I stood before Jane who sat in her drunken
chair
and screamed at her:
"I'M A GENIUS AND NOBODY KNOWS IT BUT
ME!"

she shook her head, sneered and
said,
"shit! you're a fucking
asshole!"

I stalked around the room, this time picking up a
piece of glass much larger than usual. I reached down
and plucked it out: a lovely large chunk dripping
with my blood. I flung it away, turned and glared
at Jane:
*"you don't know anything, you
whore!"*

"FUCK YOU!" she
screamed back at
me.

then the phone rang. I picked it up and announced
loudly, "I'M A GENIUS AND NOBODY KNOWS IT BUT
ME!"

it was the desk clerk: "Mr. Chinaski, I've warned you
again and again, you are keeping the other
guests awake."

"GUESTS?" I laughed back, "YOU MEAN THOSE FUCKING
WINOS?"

then Jane was at my side. she grabbed the phone and
yelled, "I'M A FUCKING GENIUS TOO AND I'M THE
ONLY WHORE WHO KNOWS IT!"

and she hung up.

I walked over and put the
chain on the door.
then Jane and I pushed the sofa in
front of the door
turned out the lights
and sat up in bed
waiting for them.
we were well aware of the
location of the drunk
tank: North Avenue 21,
such a fancy sounding
address.

we each had a chair at the
side of the bed,
and each chair held an ashtray,
cigarettes and
wine.

they arrived right on
time.
"is this the
door?"
"yeah, this is
413."

one of them beat on
the door with his night

stick:
"L.A. POLICE DEPARTMENT!
OPEN UP IN THERE!"

we did not
open up in there.

then they both beat on the door
with their night sticks:
"OPEN UP! OPEN UP IN
THERE!"

now all the guests were
awake for sure.

"come on, open up," one of them
said more gently, "we just want to
talk to you, nothing more."

"nothing more," said the other
one, "we might even join you for
a little drink."

North Avenue 21 was a terrible place,
40 or 50 men slept on the cement floor
and there was only the toilet into which nobody dared to
excrete.

"we know that you're good people, we just
want to talk,"
one of them said.

"yeah," said the other one.

then we heard them
whispering.
then a few minutes passed
but
we didn't hear them walk
away.
we were not sure that they

were gone.

"holy shit," Jane said,
"do you think they're
gone?"

"SHUSH!"
I hissed.

we sat there in the dark.
there was nothing to do
but watch the neon signs
through the window to the
east.
one was near the library
and said urgently
in red:
JESUS SAVES.
the other sign was more
interesting,
it was a large yellow bird
which flapped its wings
seven times
and then giant letters lit up
below
advertising
SIGNAL GASOLINE.

it was as good a life
as we could then
afford.

the counter revolution

waking up
in a motel room
having slept in your
shorts
alone
after a fight with
the girlfriend.

getting up
peeking
through the
venetian blinds

you're in
Hollywood
the east Kansas
City of
nowhere

slowly
you slip back
into your
body
thinking

I'm glad I
had the money
to pay for
this crap-hole
in order to
sleep off the
argument.

it beats waking
up

hungover
in a holding
cell
with a phone
on the wall
with 3 Mexicans
in there with you
who
prefer to be
called
Chicanos:
2 of the
Chicanos
on the floor
with you
the
3rd
on the telephone

he's been talking for
an hour and
30 minutes

what is there to
say that takes so
long?

he's been talking
to his
mother.

you need to make your own
phone call

but you're
white
you're
spoiled

you'll
wait.

it used to be just the
Blacks who
concentrated on your
white skin

now the
Chicanos
and everyone else
of color is
concentrating
on it too.

so it's
not so bad
right now
being in a
motel room
shower
while your
car keys and
your wallet are
safe under the
mattress.

you step out
of the motel
shower
wrap a fat white
towel
around your
fat white
body

step into
the other room

dripping wet

you see it
now
in the dresser

mirror

why they distrust
you

the Chicanos and
the Blacks.

just be glad, man, you're
not in the exercise
yard at
San Quentin
right now.

meanwhile, at the
moment
your problem is
easy and sweet:
a) dump the broad
b) go on trying.

meanwhile
you towel off
get
dressed
get
your stuff
from under the
mattress

leave the key on the
dresser
get dressed
get
out

walk down
stupid staircase
to the parking
lot

where your
auto is
still there

you and your
white skin
get into the
auto

fully paid for
it
starts
backs out

travels down the
boulevard
finds the
freeway

the driver thinking,
yes, it's o.k. that I am
white—

it might be the
result of divine
circumstance or
it might be the curse of
the devil

but that's just the way it
is

and suddenly
he thinks:
white is
beautiful, I'm
tired of
apologizing, I like my
paint job.

a definition

love is a light at
night running through the fog

love is a beercap
stepped on while on the way
to the bathroom

love is the lost key to your door
when you're drunk

love is what happens
one year in ten

love is a crushed cat

love is the old newsboy on the
corner who has
given it up

love is what you think the other
person has destroyed

love is what vanished with the
age of battleships

love is the phone ringing,
the same voice or another
voice but never the right
voice

love is betrayal
love is the burning of the
homeless in an alley

love is steel

love is the cockroach
love is a mailbox

love is rain upon the roof
of an old hotel
in Los Angeles

love is your father in a coffin
(who hated you)

love is a horse with a broken
leg
trying to stand
while 45,000 people
watch

love is the way we boil
like the lobster

love is everything we said
it wasn't

love is the flea you can't
find

and love is a mosquito

love is 50 grenadiers

love is an empty
bedpan

love is a riot in San Quentin
love is a madhouse
love is a donkey standing in a
street of flies

love is an empty barstool

love is a film of the Hindenburg
curling to pieces

a moment that still screams

love is Dostoyevsky at the
roulette wheel

love is what crawls along
the ground

love is your woman dancing
pressed against a stranger

love is an old woman
stealing a loaf of
bread

and love is a word used
too much and
much
too soon.

Gothic and etc.

I heard from two fellows who each are going to
write a thesis on Chinaski.
one is from Louisiana and the other from
somewhere in the midwest.
they both type careful letters on
expensive paper.
they sound young but interested
and I answer their letters, but
I don't say too much.

I feel that I am the geek
in their literary circus
so even though I don't say much
(so as not to disappoint them)
I do throw in a few strange lines
as if my mind was properly
unattended.

some years back
another fellow mailed me his thesis.
there were pages and pages
wherein I was given much praise:
I was the Whitman of Los Angeles
and I
was *Gothic* in addition to being
any number of other
strange and sundry things.
I was given credit for knowing
much more than I do
and he concluded by saying
I had written a few pieces that had
unmatched psychological insight.

this is what they finally do to you
after you've failed for

the first 50 years of your life
trying to get something going:
they want to give you credit for much
more than you ever
intended.

the students want it to be mysterious and
important.

I want it to be easy.

which is what it
is.

Brando

talking about
                Marlon Brando
in bed
at ten thirty in the morning
I see bamboo stalks through the window
bamboo outside the window to the north

me naked
her
in a pink nightgown

the ceiling is white
the walls are white

it has stopped raining
the sun burns in from the east

we are talking about
                Marlon Brando
at ten thirty in the morning

and the entire world
holds still
                like an orange

like a huge orange

all holds still

me naked
her
in a pink nightgown

we speak of
                Brando

then we
forget him

and he
doesn't think of
us at
all.

we get up and
eat breakfast,
satisfied.

rogue's gallery

saw this photo of
T. S. Eliot as a young man
and damn
if he didn't look just like
the fellow who used to
talk and brag
all night long
on the swing shift
at the L.A. post office
telling me how many times
he'd gotten laid that day
or that week and
how many women
he'd had to turn down.

saw this photo of
Ezra Pound
and damn
if he didn't remind me of
this skinny guy
who I once saw catch a cat
in the railroad yard
bang its head against a boxcar
kill it
skin it
in a minute-and-a-half
and then
hold the wet fur pelt up
admiring it.
this guy and Ez looked alike and
had the same goatee.

saw this photo of
F. Scott
and he reminded me of

the guy who told me
he used to spend his free time
watching the little boys
through a hole
in the crapper wall
at the Y.
"if they can't see you watching
it don't matter,"
he told me.
I maintained that it did
matter, somehow.

and H. L. Mencken's photo
reminded me
of the guy
who for some years
had been climbing
through the windows of homes
in our neighborhood
during the 1930s depression
stealing
radios, waffle irons, cans of
beans and so forth.
I watched the cops come get him.
I was 13 years old
it was high noon
and there were 4 or 5 cops
and they had the handcuffs
on him
and the sun
glittered
on the cuffs.

the photo of D. H. Lawrence
reminded me of this
sex fiend high school kid:
he got little girls
he got big girls
and then he got caught
and they took him away
only I didn't know

what he was like until
after they got him.
he was my friend.
we used to play handball
against my garage door
and he seemed to me to be
about
like anybody else.

the photo of Hemingway
I couldn't connect with
anybody.
no, come to think of
it, he reminded me
of the old bum
I gave 50 cents to
the other day.
his head wasn't quite
as round
but he did have the same white
scraggly beard but
maybe I was only thinking
that he looked like Ernie because
actually
he had pointed red elf-like
ears that
quivered as he spoke, very
fascinating—
you could see the sunlight
through them
and then he took the money
and walked away.

media

we sat around her plush
pad and
she asked me,
"how come you never got
any media attention?
you've got all this talent.
how come you wasted all
those years as
a common laborer?"

and I just sat there
with that rich and educated
lady—
I couldn't answer her
right away—
but I thought,
what could you do?
knock on doors?
what could you say to
them then?
I'd often failed even
to land a job
as a dishwasher.

so I told her,
"it never occurred
to me one way or the
other."

"it should have,"
she said. "it would
have saved you a lifetime
of agony."

soon there was a

knock on the door, and
soon another, and
they started arriving—
all of them famous:
a famous cartoonist, a
famous columnist, a
famous actor...

soon they were all there,
especially in the
patio where food was
being served.

I'm lucky to be here,
I thought, I could never
afford a place like
this.

I told the lady that
I wished to retire
early
and I took a
fifth of imported
whiskey to the bedroom,
had a few drinks
in the dark
then got undressed
crawled into her bed
switched on
the cable TV
and watched it
and waited.

after the lady went
to work the next
morning
I got into my car
and drove slowly down
out of those
Hollywood Hills
knowing I'd never

go there again.

I went back
to town
to my apartment
with the busted front
window
and I went inside
locked the door
got a tall
can of beer
from the refriger-
ator
opened it
had a hit
sitting there at
10:30 a.m.
on that
derelict couch and

it was one of the
best beers
I ever
tasted.

I was wrong

I bet the wrong horse.

my girl is on the rag and
my beard is turning white.

tonight I walked across the
room and ripped the nail off
my little toe. a thick mahogany
chair leg did it.

I laughed then with the temple-burners
and the polishers of
prose.

I bet the wrong horse.

the hawk got flushed down the
toilet.

the pimp scratched his fleas.

the cook dropped in celery and
carrots and potatoes and
a bone for the
dog.

I bet the wrong horse.

I'd rather be
in Jamaica
than to be sitting here tonight
typing fawns into hard
fact.

2

*an apology is no more than a
weak excuse
so I'm not going to apologize
because this poem is so short
and has no title
as I sit drinking steamed coffee from
Switzerland
while listening to that old
crybaby
Peter Ilich
Tchaikovsky.*

up, down and all around

I sometimes get edgy
wonder where I'm at,
miss a step or two, feel
lost.

everybody I know seems
taller
more intelligent
kinder
than I am
and
of course
not as
ugly.

but that mood never
lasts
very long.

I take a good
look around,
a straight
hard look around
and then
I know
better

but just
for a
while.

the main course

Jesus Christ, he tells me, Rita and I have split,
just general attrition and general unhappiness.
anyhow, I've been eating out and it's like having
the same bad dream over and over again.

whatcha mean? I ask.

I mean, he tells me, I keep going to different restaurants
but it's the same everywhere,
the same dim lights and empty tables.
I go in, you know, but no matter where I go
the same man gets up from his newspaper and
comes to my table ...

hands you a menu? I say.

yes, and I am pleased for him: I am bringing him
money, I am bringing him trade ...

he might fail otherwise?

I don't know, he continues. anyhow, I order a beer,
soup, salad, shrimp and fries.
I make a small joke, hand him back the menu.
he walks off to the kitchen.
outside, it rains; inside, music plays
on the radio.

then? I ask.

the soup arrives. not too bad. I read the paper,
spoon the soup
and the paper says things like:
WOMAN STEALS BABY FROM MOTHER FOR
3 MONTHS.

HORSE MEAT FROM AUSTRALIA BEING SERVED
AT NATIONWIDE CHAIN OF FAST-FOOD
RESTAURANTS.
MAN KILLS ESTRANGED WIFE, 3 CHILDREN AND
STRANGER WHO HAPPENED TO BE
READING THE GAS METER.

then? I ask.

then the salad comes. it's not bad.

the only good salad, I say, I haven't
eaten yet.

I finish the salad. then comes the
main course. fair. somewhat dry and
tasteless.

you eat it? I ask.

yeah, he says, only I need help. I call him over
again. another beer, please.

then?

he brings it then
goes and sits by the cash register.
he waits.
I am finished eating.
I nod.
he comes back and lays the bill on
the table.
he goes back to the register.
he sits down.

he is not important, I say.
why do you think about
him? you're letting him rob you of your
peace.

I leave him a tip anyhow, he says.

and then?

then I get up.
pay.
leave.

well, you've eaten.

yes. and when I go to another cafe
and then to cafe after cafe,
this same man gets up from his
newspaper, moves to my table and takes
my order!

sometimes things never change, I suggest.
sometimes things stay the same.

he'll always be waiting there in the dim light, he says,
waiting for me!
pretending to be someone he's not!

but he doesn't love or hate you, I
say, he doesn't even know your name.

but it's like having the same nightmare, he says,
over and over again!
when is it going to stop?

when things get dark, I say, even after we awake,
sometimes things are worse than ever before.

I gotta begin eating in, he
says.

it's all music

the girl in the fish market stands with her back to
me.
she's dressed in a brown smock and has long golden
hair.
I'm down at the docks and there are fish everywhere.
many of the fish are large and seem to be almost
alive as their
eyes look up at me.

a man steps out of an ice locker holding a
huge silver fish by its open mouth as
the girl in the fish market turns and looks at me.
I ask her to cut me a swordfish steak.

driving back to town the fish is on the seat
next to me
wrapped in pink paper that is only a little lighter
than the color of the pink fish.

I drive back to my house
up the driveway and
park the car in the garage.

I walk into the house
where the woman I live with is talking
on the telephone.
she spends her days talking
on the telephone
and it's best for both of us that she does.

I take the fish out of the pink paper and put
it carefully in the refrigerator.
then I go upstairs to where I can be myself
and listen to the *Mass*
in B Minor by
Johann Sebastian Bach.

my cat, the writer

as I sit at this
machine
my cat Ting sits behind
me
on the back of my
chair.

now
as I type
he
steps on the edge of an open
drawer
and then out on the
desk itself.

now
his nose is dangerously close
to the flying keys
as he watches me
type.

then
he backs off
goes
over and sticks his nose into
a
coffee cup.

now
he's back
his head brushing the edge
of this unfinished
poem.
as
he

sticks his paw down into the
guts of the
machine.

I
hit a key and
he
leaps away.

then
he just sits and once again watches me
type.

I've moved my wine glass and
bottle
to the other side of
the
machine.

the radio plays bad
piano
music.

Ting just sits and continues to watch
me
type.

do you think he wants to be
a
writer?
or was he one in a past
life?

I
dislike cute cat
poems
but now
I've written one.

suddenly
there's a fly in

here
and Ting watches its every
move.

it's 1:45 a.m. now and
I'm
sleepy.

listen, relax, I'm sure
you've read
worse
poems than
this

and I've written
worse
too.

one for the road

It's not sad to think of Socrates
taking hemlock;
in those days it was a simple choice:
in or out.
in our time, within this confused
superstructure,
I can see him as just another
old drunk at the bar
on a Saturday afternoon,
far more interesting than most
of course
but just as helpless as he
confronted the compounded
wisdom of the
centuries.
he'd probably just go out and
get laid the best he
could
and like the rest of us
try to survive the
coming
night.

room 22

I've always liked old hotels with stairs that
squeak
old hotels run by indifferent managers who enjoy
renting you,
for example,
room 22—

opening the battered window for
the first time
the fumes from the avenue below
rush up deadly as
you stand at the window
and watch the traffic signal change:
red yellow green
green yellow red.

the second floor is best:
in case of fire
only two broken legs
and another chance at life's
game.

old hotels like old women
become better
more mellow
more human
because there's nothing else
left for them to do.

it's the same in St. Louis,
Kansas City or L.A.

sitting down on the sagging mattress
you think of the many people
who have lived in that room

who are now probably dead, and you wonder
how many people actually died there
in that room.

but there's a charm, a definite
charm there
as you sit on the bed
thinking, you've got a whole week
ahead of you
and almost ten dollars left over.
that can be as safe as you will
ever get.

soon there will be a knock on the door,
usually a toothless old guy
waving a near-empty bottle of
cheap wine.

"come in," you'll say.

and he will be all right
he will talk better sense than
your father or the college professors
but, of course, they wouldn't agree
because he's without a job or
money.

I like my new room
I like the dripping faucet,
I like the toilet down the hall
I like my old guest
and soon there's another knock and
there's another old guy
and then another knock
a woman
not too old
she brings some vodka.

soon
everybody is talking
smoking cigarettes

they come in and go out as they
use the bathroom
down the hall.

somebody turns on your radio
and soon everybody is talking LOUD.
it's nice in room
22.

somebody pukes in my
sink.

a fist fight starts between two
70-year-old men.
I
stop it.

I look up and see the hotel
manager
she's been drinking too, holding a
cigarette in her mouth
she tells us to quiet down,
the long grey ash about to drop
and fall into the front of her gown.

then later
to awaken alone
in a roomful of empty bottles and silent
dried puke
discarded food and candy wrappers
scattered on the floor and
rug.

you get up
dress
go down the squeaking stairs
buy a newspaper
come back up
take off your shoes
climb onto the bed
and read the

Help Wanted section
looking for someone
who needs a
shipping clerk
stockboy
busboy
dishwasher.

those old hotels
they give a man a chance
as long as he can enjoy
a few good nights in
room 22.

she caught it on the fly

the entertainer smokes 50 dollar cigars
and goes out on stage and sings
and the women throw panties at him.
some of the panties come out of their
purses and some of them actually come
off their bodies.
he sings love songs and that's what
they want, and he wiggles a bit and
he sweats.
I'd hardly compare him to Sinatra
but he seems an all right sort—
he generates a certain electricity, and if
he was my gardener or my mechanic
I'd probably like him.

I know an airline stewardess
who told me: "he's a pig. he took
a stewardess into the crapper while
we were in flight and he fucked her.
she got the clap. all my feeling
for him has left me."

there you go: love gone wrong again.
this is where we live and it keeps
happening.

I've never had the clap but if I were
bombarded with all those panties I
probably would have had it several
times.

and I don't think it has hurt
his singing. and that's what they're
paying for.

a drink to that

we were on LaBrea Ave. and I asked her,
"want to see the house I lived in for
15 years when I was a boy?"
"sure," she said.
I drove over to Longwood Ave. and we
parked across the street.
there it was 50 years later
it was still there
the house of horrors
the house of a thousand beatings
the house of brutality and unhappiness.
"show me where your bedroom was,"
she said.
we walked across the lawn
the lawn I had mowed and watered
750 times.
we walked up the neighbor's driveway.
"there it is," I told her, "there is the
window I crawled out of at night, and
I think that's the same bush I slid over.
Christ, let's get out of here!"
we got back into the car and drove off.
I had been the victim of no love from
either parent. and I had been the victim
of much more than that. and the luck had
held bad for a long long time
thereafter.

"you didn't want to see that house again,
did you?" she asked.
"it was my idea," I said. "I'm sorry."
"Baby," she said, "I'm sorry too."
"it's over," I said, "some of it is
over."

105

when we got back to my place and
opened the door
the angels jumped out of the wastebaskets
and ran across the worn, brown
rug
light and luck were bouncing from the
walls as
she went to the bathroom
while I kicked back and
popped a bottle of Havemeyer
Bernkastel Riesling.

sit and endure

well, first Mae West died
and then George Raft,
and Eddie G. Robinson's
been gone
a long time,
and Bogart and Gable
and Grable,
and Laurel and
Hardy
and the Marx Brothers,
all those Saturday
afternoons
at the movies
as a boy
are gone now
and I look
around this room
and it looks back at me
and then out through
the window.
time hangs helpless
from the doorknob
as a gold
paperweight
of an owl
looks up at me
(an old man now)
who must sit and endure
these many empty
Saturday
afternoons.

out of the money

there is this superstar jockey who has taken a
sudden interest in the written word and one night
at my place he asked me,
"listen, isn't there something I can read?" I told him,
"well, there's this fellow Céline, he wrote a book called
Journey to the End of the Night."

a couple of nights later
he phoned.
"listen, I can't find that book in any of the stores";
so I told him where he might find
Céline.
I met him at the track one day and asked,
"did you find that book yet?"
and he said, "yeah."
each time I saw him at the track after that
I asked,
"you read that book yet?"
"no," he'd answer.

the last time he told me, "I couldn't get into it. it was
too slow."
"what?" I said.
"yeah," he said. "I gave the book to my wife."
"good," I said. "well?"
"she said it was depressing."

I played out the card and then drove home, thinking,
he can't be talking about Céline, not the Céline I read
that rainy winter night
so many years ago
after a long day at the Acme Electric Co. spent
packing light fixtures
into wooden crates.
reading Céline for the first time there in my

room
I laughed out loud at the crazy truth
bounced on the springs
turned and beat the mattress with my
fist, thinking, nobody can write like
this, this is the beginning and the middle
and the end of it
all!

I still see that jockey at the track
now and then, he's a
good sort, but
it doesn't quite mean the same thing
to me.
we just talk about the
horses and let it go
at that.

4 cops

dogs walk the walls
as the submarine sinks quickly to the
bottom.

I sit in a coffee shop
with 32 cardboard faces
most of them blank.

4 very fine cops
sit at a table
watching me.

I guess
I don't look so
good to them.

why didn't we get
those boys killed
in some war?
their mothers would only
have cried for
ten minutes.

I've been packed
(in here) for
seven decades: no
front, no back, no top,
no bottom.
my parents wanted me
to succeed in some curious
profession
that only they
could understand.

my life unfolds in front of me
like a dirty napkin.
I'll never come back to this coffee shop
again.

my girlfriend says it's all so easy

"she designs the sets for Broadway plays and edits art
films. he plays the flamenco guitar, he's really
famous and has his hands insured for 200
thousand dollars."

"he makes customized hot-tubs and when winter
comes he works at the best ski resorts. she makes lovely
baskets and sells them at craft fairs. she's
really very talented."

"he takes the photographs while she interviews
celebrities. they built their beachfront home themselves
with stones they found along the shore."

"he grows grass in Hawaii and smuggles it into L.A.
in surfboards. she writes for a famous pop music
magazine."

"she restores pleasure boats and he
manages a rock group and arranges all their tours.
they have a brilliant child."

"she only works a couple of months a year as
an income tax consultant and he buys and
sells houses. he'll buy a house for
500 thousand and he'll sell it for 600 thousand
4 months later."

"he'll only take odd jobs, he makes enough in
3 or 4 days to lay around for a month or more.
she does wood carving, she's really good."

"his father died and now he runs the lumber
company. he used to be gay and an
alcoholic. she's so *tiny*, and half his

size. they finally got married."

"they live in Mexico and South America.
they know how to live off the land.
they make jewelry and sell it not only to
the tourists but also to the natives. he never
learned to speak English. he doesn't have to.
he just sits there and looks at you with
those eyes! oh, my god!"

"he goes to Spain every year and lives
in a castle. he has an English accent and
the women are crazy about him."

jesus christ, I think of all the factories and
the warehouses where I worked,
the park benches on which I slept, the
jails I've been in and then to hear about all
these others!

I could have made wood carvings or lounged in
art school or traveled to Crete or
stretched skins in Peru or I could have
wept at the feet of rich old ladies or
constructed handmade crossbows for the
hunting of boar!

it's all so easy
all you've got to do
is to be
clever and bright

if I hadn't been retarded
I could have been
like them:

the handy and successful magic people
everywhere!

American Literature II

personal is best. I know this professor,
we were drinking beer together and he
said, "I don't see how you can be so personal
in your writing, isn't it embarrassing?"

he's wrong, it's all personal.
history is personal. pulling a shade up
in the morning is personal. drinking beer is. the
abstract is. the objective is. the waterbug
is, and synapse is.

and nothing is more personal than walking down
a stairway alone
thinking about nothing. I often like to
think about nothing for hours.

this professor, he'd simply taught too long
while I'd been a night watchman and a
circus hand. there was really nothing I could
tell him but I tried: "drink your beer,"
I told him, "and tell me about your
wife."

he would only drink his beer so
I told him about my wife.

heartache

I was living in this gay hotel,
he told me.
it was getting to me.
I began fucking those guys.
I even fell in love with a drag queen.
well, the other morning I found a
dildo in the trash can, it was still
coated with vaseline. I just hadda get
out of Frisco so I flew down to San Diego.
I'm in this bar and I meet this young
girl, marvelous body. we drink awhile
and she says she'll suck my cock (she sucks
so she won't get pregnant).
we go to her place and I find out there
are 3 guys in the front room. I ask her
who they are. and she says, oh, they
are my lovers. and I say, wait a minute,
you mean to tell me you suck those 3
cocks too? she says yes and I get out of
there.
I go to do a painting of an attorney. he
promised me $300 and when I finished he
said, I'll give you $25.
what the hell, I said, that doesn't even
cover the costs of paints and paper, let
alone my soul.

$25, he says.

I ripped up the painting and
walked out.
now I don't know what to do.
maybe I'll go back to
New York.
where do you think I ought

to go?

Portland, I said.

Portland! he said, furious. Don't
fuck with my head! where'd you get
that hanging plant? what are you
doing with a cat? and who painted your
bathroom that awful
color?

I cause some remarkable creativity

she burned holes in the couch with her
cigarettes
drank almost a 5th of scotch by 2 p.m.
and turned the radio up
very loud
to the symphony.
she got very intellectual
and her idea of intellectual
was to disagree with everything
said by me,
also
she wasn't very good in bed
so I wearied of it all and told her it was
over.

now she phones me continually.
long distance.
she reads me poems she's written.

there's one about a fly
even a fly can feel pain,
says the poem.

there's another about how she killed a
june bug. there's no law against killing a
june bug,
says the poem.

then she phones and tells me that she has
submitted a story to a magazine
and in it she exposes
me.

do you want me to read you the story?
she asks.

no, it's all right, I say, and
hang up.

there's another lady I know who wrote a long
        unpleasant
story
about how she killed a roach with her
bare foot.

I should introduce them.

the cosmic joke

men and women finally break.
men and women
deliberately abandon their
loved ones in madhouses
sedated or
electrified
until they die.

cats kill cats at
3 a.m. in the morning
chewing off the front
legs and opening the
throat
leaving stiffened fur
and still forms
for any collector of
garbage and life
past gone.

so many wish to be kind
and understanding
so many wish to act educated
and knowing
so many use the word
love
as if they meant
it.

and too many believe it
when they hear
it.

our chances are negated
by our very desire to
be kind.

we've got to raise taxes
so we can feed and
clothe and amuse
all those
in madhouses
and elsewhere
who believed in love
when there was so
little
there.

the death of the snowman

the only time it ever snowed in
Los Angeles
we made a little snowman in Neal's
front yard, the only snowman
any of us had ever
seen: raisins for eyes,
carrot for nose,
wine cork in mouth
like a cigar.
that was at 8 a.m. in the
morning.
by the time noon
came around
all the snow had melted
from the roofs and the
lawns
but our snowman was still
there
only he was getting
smaller.
Neal decided that we should
put him in his parents'
icebox so he would stop
melting
so we did.

the next day the snowman
was still in the icebox
there on the back porch
and he was only a little
smaller.
he reminded us of the miracle
that had happened.
there were four of us:

Neal, me, Eddie and Gene.
we reached in and touched him
and admired him.
we knew it would probably
never snow again in Los
Angeles.

it was 3 or 4 days after
that
one afternoon
we were out in front
when Neal
yelled, "THEY'VE GOT OUR
SNOWMAN!"

we didn't know those guys,
they weren't even from our
school.
one of them had the snowman
and was running around
and around in
Neal's backyard
like he didn't know
where to go with it;
there was a high fence
back there.
there was the guy with the
snowman
and three other guys
all about our age.
we ran back and started
swinging at them.
the guy with the snowman
dropped it and started
swinging back.
they were good fighters
but we knew we were right
and we were madder
and so they started losing
and getting bloody

noses.
even though they cussed
better than we did,
we backed them off.
three of the guys started
running
but the biggest of them
the fourth guy
reached down
grabbed the head off our
little snowman and stuck it
into his mouth.
"KILL HIM!" Neal yelled.
we went for him
but he ran off
up the driveway
he had really long legs
and we couldn't catch
him.

we walked back to what
was left of our snowman.
we'd stepped all over him
during the fight.
there wasn't much left.
small dirty white chunks.
"no use saving this,"
Neal said.
and he started crushing
and stamping the snowman
into the ground.
soon there was just a
bit of wet earth.

"how'd those pricks
find out about
our snowman?" Neal asked.

•

we were sitting around when
Neal's mother came home.
she went in the house for a while,
then she came out on
the back porch.

"what happened to the
snowman?" she asked.

"nuthin'," Neal answered.

"don't talk to me in that
tone of voice!"
she said.

Neal just sat there.

"did you hear what I said,
Neal?"

"yeah ..."

"there you go again!
you come into the house
this minute!"

Neal got up and walked
into the house.
Eddie, Gene and me
got up
and we walked out to the
street
and Gene went off to where
he lived
and Eddie went to where
he lived
and I went to where
I lived
and we didn't say

anything,
we didn't even say
goodbye.
we knew it would
never snow in Los Angeles
again.

shut out

they were putting the horses in the gate and I
was rushing to get my bet down and there were two
men ahead of me in the line.
the first, a well-dressed fellow, seemed to be
leaning up against the window and dozing.
"JESUS CHRIST," I yelled "SLEEP AT HOME!"

"LOOK AT HIM," I said to the man in front of
me, "HE'S TRYING TO PICK UP HIS TICKETS WITH ONE
      HAND!"

"yes, he's very slow," said the man in front
of me.

"I'VE SEEN SOME JERK-OFFS IN MY DAY!" I said loudly,
"BUT THIS BABY BEATS THEM ALL!"

the man at the window slowly picked up his tickets,
turned around and said to me, "buddy, I've only
got one arm."

"sorry, sir," I said. then as an afterthought
I said, "listen, if you've
only got one arm you ought to make your bets way
ahead of time!"

he walked off and the bell rang
sending them out of the gate and there was
nothing to do then but go back to the bar.

the machine gunner

some have compared my typewriter to a machine gun,
even I have,
but sometimes I run out of bullets
and I cover it (the gun)
and walk into the bedroom
fall on the bed
and think,
god almighty, why did I ever quit my job
as a stockboy at Sears Roebuck?
they had such nice little smocks and gave me a
ten percent discount on purchases.

there's no response from the hinterlands
to my immortal stories, the editors sit on them like
pillows.
the only thing that arrives are the poets
they must have a rotating schedule.
"come on, Chinaski, let's drink and talk!
you're lonely, Chinaski, you're getting
paranoid ..."
"no, listen," I say, "believe me, there's a different gang here
every night. even a crew with a tape recorder
last night. it was awful!"
"ah, I bet you loved it! have another
drink!"

they even sleep here and in the morning I tell them
they must go. they don't understand.
they tell me I can live by my name alone; they tell me I
don't realize who I now am. I know who I
am.

after they leave, it's the mailbox.
no replies from the magazines. only personal letters
that want answering: a letter from Israel, a letter from

New York, 2 letters from San Diego, one from New Orleans
and one from Normal, Illinois. between the poets
and the personal letters I *am* immortal,
but who's tending the store?
where's the machine gun?
I've fought a lifetime to be able to write
and now I'm running a correspondence course and an
all-night bar.

I've got to get an old woman to guard that door
and answer the phone:
"I'm sorry but Mr. Chinaski is indisposed today.
would you care to leave a
message?"

of course, they'll call me a son-of-a-bitch.
well, I am.
or they're making me into
one.

2 deaths

you told me many years ago
(long before Stravinsky died
today)
that you wanted to learn
everything
about engines and buildings
and war and women
and cities
and the history of
Man
and I told you
it's tiresome
don't bother
what counts is not what we
know
but what we don't
know.

you wanted so desperately to prove that you could
know what was not already
known.

and when I saw you in your
casket I had no idea that
Stravinsky would also die
today
and that I would sit here
and write about both of you
tonight.

schoolyards of forever

the schoolyard was a horror show: the bullies, the
freaks
the beatings up against the wire fence
our schoolmates watching
glad that they were not the victim;
we were beaten well and good
time after time
and afterwards were
followed
taunted all the way home where often
more beatings awaited us.

in the schoolyard the bullies ruled well,
and in the restrooms and
at the water fountains they
owned and disowned us at will
but in our own way we held strong
never begged for mercy
we took it straight on
silently
we were toughened by that horror
a horror that would later serve us in good stead
and then strangely
as we grew stronger and bolder
the bullies gradually began to back off.

grammar school
jr. high
high school
we grew up like odd neglected plants
gathering nourishment where we could
blossoming in time
and later when the bullies tried to befriend us
we turned them away.

then college
where under a new regime
the bullies melted almost entirely away
we became more and they became much less.

but there were new bullies now
the professors
who had to be taught the hard lessons we'd learned
we glowed madly
it was grand and easy
the coeds dismayed at our gamble
and our nerve
but we looked right through them
to the larger fight waiting out there.

then when we arrived *out there*
it was back up against the fence
new bullies once again
deeply entrenched by society
bosses and the like
who kept us in our place for decades to come
so we had to begin all over again
in the street
and in small rooms of madness
rooms that were always dim at noon
it lasted and lasted for years like that
but our former training enabled us to endure
and after what seemed like
an eternity
we finally found the tunnel at the end of the light.

it was a small enough victory
no songs of braggadocio because
we knew we had won very little from very little,
and that we had fought so hard to be free
just for the simple sweetness of it.

but even now we still can see the grade school janitor
with his broom
and sleeping face;
we can still see the little girls with their curls

their hair so carefully brushed and shining
in their freshly starched dresses;

see the faces of the teachers
fat folded forlorn;

hear the bell at recess;
see the grass and the baseball diamond;
see the volleyball court and its white net;
feel the sun always up and shining there
spilling down on us like the juice of a giant tangerine.

and we did not soon forget
Herbie Ashcroft
our principal tormentor
his fists as hard as rocks
as we crouched trapped against the steel fence
as we heard the sounds of automobiles passing but not stopping
and as the world went about doing what it does
we asked for no mercy
and we returned the next day and the next and the next
to our classes
the little girls looking so calm and secure
as they sat upright in their seats
in that room of blackboards and chalk
while we hung on grimly to our stubborn disdain
for all the horror and all the strife
and waited for something better
to come along and comfort us
in that never-to-be-forgotten
grammar school world.

beaujolais jadot

the dogs of Belgium feel bad
on certain winter afternoons
as
the sweep of things goes
this way or that.
nothing, nobody is ever spared.

no matter, tragedy
continually reminds us of random
chance:
great airliners crash into unseen
mountain ranges;
old ladies set themselves
on fire
smoking lonely cigarettes in
forgotten rooming houses;
small wars continue, and brutal rapes,
and there is always accidental murder
as the dogs of Belgium feel bad
on
certain winter afternoons:
their eyes show it, they
twitch and shiver—
and there's no place to go, there's
never a place to go, it's meant to be
that way.
sitting here like this,
wondering about it all, with
beaujolais jadot
spilled across the desk,
all I can think
of are
the dogs of Belgium,
and Christ, they must be feeling
awful bad to get inside my head

like this.

maybe it doesn't mean anything
at all, that would be
best.
across from where I sit
is another room
and
soon I will go in there and
I will stretch out on the bed
and sleep a dreamless sleep
and
thus I will escape
those dogs of Belgium
who would continually remind me of
the lost and forsaken
lives of so
many.

bar chatter

Arnold looked down into his drink and
said, "when you finally realize that
there is no one
perfect woman, then you can wait
on death in a settled fashion instead
of being tricked into the usual frenzy
caused by the ladies."

Mike looked down into his drink and
answered, "but, to establish
sanity you must first endure a series of
insanities."

"the insanities," said Arnold. "I remember
all their names ..."

"I remember," said Mike, "that they all
were similar: intestines, elbows, skulls,
ears, kneecaps, veins, hair, eyes, noses,
feet, toes and so forth ..."

"I remember their complaints best," said
Arnold. "none of them seemed to like
me."

"they liked you," Harry answered, "but they
were trying to mold you into
their vision ..."

"let's not talk about women," Arnold said.
"it doesn't lead anywhere."

"all right then," said Mike, "let's try
this one: how long do you think we
have before a nuclear war wipes us

out?"

"god damn, man," said Arnold, "from
women to nuclear war!"

"hey," said Mike, "look at *that* one who
just walked in! I'll bet her intestines
are in great shape!"

they watched her walk to her bar stool and
sit down.

then they began to talk
about professional football.
they both liked the game, it was sensible,
brutal and brave
and talking about it
they began to feel less worse
and much much
better

and as they talked
the woman with the great intestines
blew a perfect smoke ring
about the shape and size of a
baboon's asshole.

she stuck her finger through it
as Harold and Arnold ordered
another round.
they didn't have much time
left now at
all.

punched-out

I remember best coming out of that factory into the
night
none of us saying much
glad to get out
but needing the job
—getting into our old cars
one could hear the grinding of the starters
the sudden roar and explosions as
the worn engines fired up once more
—as we backed wearily
out of the parking lot
to pull away
leaving the factory back there
—each of us to a different place
—some to a wife and children
—others to empty rented rooms or to
small crowded apartments:
as for me
I never knew if my woman would be there or
not
or how drunk she would be
if she was home
—but for each of us
the factory waited back there
our timecards punched and neatly
racked.

for me somehow
the best time was that moment
driving from the factory to where I lived
stopping at the signals
looking at the crowds
suspended
between a place I didn't want to be
and a place I didn't want to go

—I was caught between my two unhappy lives
but so were most of the others there
not only from that warehouse
in that city
but in the world
entire:
we had no chance
yet still we all managed to continue and
endure.

counterpoint

he noticed that every time he
expressed an opinion she
contradicted him.

he decided to ignore it.
that is, he decided not to mention it to
her.

but each time he expressed an opinion
(as the days and weeks went by)
she quickly contradicted him.

he thought, it's probably her way of
asserting her intelligence.
she probably does it to
everyone.

he decided to keep his opinions to himself
and to speak out less
or not at all
if possible.

but one day
he slipped up and
expressed an opinion and
she contradicted him again.

so he decided to mention it to her.
he said, "do you realize that every time
I express an opinion you
contradict me?"

"why, that's not true!" she
replied.

3 pairs of panties

Sweden is a lousy place
Paris is a lousy place

the executioner cut off the
wrong heads

when you left
you left behind
3 pairs of panties
and I'm too fat to
wear them

London is a lousy place

Los Angeles is a lousy place
now:
dank clicking beast
dead fish memory stalking
me,
ambulances masquerading as flower petals:

what was wrong was not
understood
and what was right didn't
last.

this drunk

this drunk in the next apartment
he looks at baseball, football, and spy dramas on
TV,
he brings home 2 or 3 women a year
I hear him through the thin walls:
"come on, baby, let me put this god-damned thing
in there!"

he also falls out of bed about 4 a.m. every morning
then he falls out of bed about 5 a.m.
and sometimes again at 6 a.m.

he's worse than a church chime.

when we had that earthquake 2 years ago
it was 6 a.m.
and I thought he had fallen out of bed again
but when the walls kept shaking
I got out of bed along with everybody else
and went outside and smoked cigarettes
and waited for the world to end.

when I saw the drunk at noon
I asked him how he liked the earthquake and
he said, "what earthquake?"

one day the drunk went out
and the landlord went in there and
started cleaning his place.

empty beer cans and bottles came
flying out, some by themselves
others in paper sacks.

it was an afternoon in October

and I stood outside and watched the cans and
bottles bounce on the
sidewalk

and then stiff and yellow
here came a Christmas tree.

I thought you might like to know about him,
he's a colorful fellow,
this drunk next door.

Casablanca

Bogie smoked 4 packs of cigarettes
a day
and was in a few good movies.

he made them good by being
in them.

some men have this undeniable
presence and some
women too.

Bogie had it.

you listened when he spoke.

which is more than my women do.

all my women say the same thing
to me: "listen, I've heard
all that before."

"heard it where?"

"from you."

Bogie had the delivery, it never
varied.
sometimes my voice changes
sometimes I sound like a callow
youth
although I don't feel like
one.

I rehearse my voice,
I practice, I

put a steel edge on my vocal
inflection:

"listen, you whore, I've *had* it
with you!"

"oh, go to sleep," they say turning
over in the bed. "I
need my rest."

Bogie with his 4 packs of smokes,
he had an instinct, a presence, even
his clothing and his demeanor were
like a gentle smirk.

and with the telling lift of an
eyebrow and those hollow
cheeks
he looked like he
knew everything.

throughout all my relationships I've tried
to be like that.

I mean, aren't we all influenced by
somebody?

I wonder
if he had lived
what he would look like
now:

smoking a pipe
in a house on a hill
sitting on a front porch
staring off at
nothing over the
rooftops
of a small town in
Arkansas

a truly terrible and
beautiful end ...

•

"this is Bogart Week on TV,"
I tell my woman.
"just think, a Bogie movie
each night for
seven nights!

"this is trash night,"
she says, "have you
taken the trash out
yet?"

I cup my hands
light a cigarette
inhale
look at her
narrow my eyes
while
gently exhaling smoke
from my mouth and my
nose:

"you take it."

the saddest words I ever heard

I was a substitute carrier
at the P.O.
and the supervisor
was out to break me
sending me out on the
toughest routes in the city
during the day
and then assigning me to
night pick-up runs.

in between
I drank and fought with
my shack job.

one afternoon coming in so tired
I could hardly
walk
there was Ernie
the assistant soup
at the desk.
he wasn't as bad as
the supervisor
and he looked up and
saw me
lit a cigarette
smiled sympathetically and
said, "I know it's
tough … but for dumb guys
like you and me
this kind of shit is
the only job
available."

then he leaned forward and
began on some paper

work.

I walked to my route case
thought about that
thought about that some more
dropped my mail sack
with a sigh
and
sat down.

the light

he won't die. 95 years old. he walks down the hill,
the very steep hill, to fetch his own groceries. then
he walks back with the big bag, leaning heavily on his
cane.

old Charlie. he won't let anybody
help him.

his is the biggest house on the hill, twelve rooms.
must be worth $500,000.00.

his wife, also 95, is in a nursing home.
he walks over to see her a few times a week.

"she looks good but she doesn't know who I am."

Charlie's children don't come around.

"they're waiting for me to die. I'll live on
to spite them!"

he used to watch television downstairs with his
wife. now he watches upstairs in another room.

"can't go in that room. it reminds me of her."

that's all there is.
he lives on bacon and cornflakes. he looks good.
he's 6-foot-two, thin, arrow-straight.

the mailman tells me, "you know that old man
next door? he's got a sharp mind."

old Charlie. 95. he won't die.

everybody he knew is dead now except his wife
who doesn't know who he is.

for a man backed into a corner he's majestic,
and when death comes it better come humbly
for this one.

I see the light shining in his upstairs room each
night.

it's the brightest metaphor for courage I've seen for
some decades.

the closing of the bottomless bar

the idea that moral outrage only
can be felt by
the gifted and the noble and the
intelligent and
the sensitive and the
powerful
that is the biggest joke of
all.
they raided the nudie bar last night,
had a Supreme Court order in their back pocket,
were
backed by the highest court in the land
and they swept the girls off the bartops
like dead flies
like dirty napkins,
all those poor lovelies screaming
in panic
their voluptuous rears twisted in surprise,
they swept them off and away
half-dressed into vans and automobiles
to be booked, fingerprinted, photographed
and jailed. such a
waste. what a waste of grade-a
goods. speak about indecency
the cops were the most indecent things there
that night. a poor girl can't make an honest
buck anymore. all they were doing was offering a
horny evening to a few lonely men. I've just got to
believe those Supreme Court boys
don't care about anything real and just
can't get it up
anymore.
listen, girls, we'll find a way, we'll bail you
out, we'll think of something.

the human body ain't no crime,
anyway, not those bodies
of yours.

fame of a sort

I dream of being
famous.
I dream of walking
down the streets
of London and Paris.
I dream of sitting
in sidewalk cafes
drinking fine wine
and taking a taxi
back to the best
hotel where
I dream of meeting
beautiful ladies
in the hall.

I'd like to see
the city of my birth,
Andernach, Germany,
explore it
then fly on to
Moscow to check out
their rapid transit system
so I'll have something
to tell the mayor
of Los Angeles
when I get back home
where I will
have dinner with him
and his family
while
feeling his wife's
legs
under the table.

never look

that's the secret: don't look.

"you never look directly at people," a girlfriend
used to say to me.
I had good reason, I didn't want to see what was actually
there, I felt better without that
reality.

I could give hundreds of examples of what I mean
but I'll just describe a
few:
say, if I boarded a jet and I saw the pilot's
untroubled and unfocused face
then it would be a very uneasy flight for me
indeed.
or say, at a harness race, if I looked into the dead eyes
of the driver who was to guide the horse of my
choice
then I'd know that I could never
bet that horse.
or say, if by chance on TV
I see a close-up of the face of the
winner of a beauty contest
I am almost always
horrified.
finally, I know it's a terrible thing to say but
when I see hundreds of human faces gathered at a sporting
event I become dizzy with nausea and
disbelief.

I appear to be misplaced among the multitudes, I don't
belong.

I am best alone watching my three cats, they are
for me

pure examples of real
life.

I can
look
without
fear
at
them.

now the professors

now the professors come with their little 6-packs of
beer and sit on my couch and talk
Literature.

"Chinaski," the professors tell me, "you get
this profound sense of total Realism into your
work."

"uh," I say,
"huh."

it was not Moyamensing Prison
it was not
not being in the War—any one of them—
it was not the railroad track gangs
the slaughterhouses
it was not the whores and Literature and
Poesy which
killed me, it was not the
landladies
it was not the fine ladies who never fucked me because I was a
bum, it was not all the bad and cheap
wine, it was
nothing—
I was neither Villon getting his ass kicked out of Paris
forever
nor was I Crane jumping into a boat propellor and/or a
shark's mouth.

it was not
sitting behind dark ripped shades
pulled down for
weeks
months
years

afraid of the landlady's footstep—
death was nothing next to that—
it was
being more and more startled by the world and
the world's people.
it was the cosmic
joke, a dirty
one at
that.

nothing has changed; it doesn't matter that
now the professors come with their little 6-packs of
beer. and *sometimes* I am lucky—once
one came along while I had the
Asian flu.
he had a little 6-pack
smiled
uttered the magic
word:
"Chinaski?"

"yeh," I said, "got the Asian flu, don't get
too close."

"ooh, what'll I do with the
beer?"

"I'll take
it."

I took the beer while he stood there under my rented
porch light
autographing his latest
expensive
hardbound
privately printed
poems.

the poems I knew
about—I didn't have to read
them. I just put the book in with all the others like

that. I had a bookcase full of
them.

the beer?

it could have been
better.

I drank it
anyhow.

the hatchet job

a) he sat across from me.

b) he said: "I will destroy Ginsberg."

c) I thought: this man is crazy.

d) he continued: "I will write a critical essay and destroy
   Ginsberg forever; he has gotten away with his nonsense for too
   long."

e) I thought: this man is very unhappy and
   envious.

f) he went on: "I will bury him."

g) I asked: "do you think he's worse than
   you or me?"

h) he countered: "yes, he is, he has a vast and
   insidious influence, and he's a fucking
   phoney."

i) I told him: "let's talk about something
   else."

j) he asked: "like what?"

k) I pleaded: "like *anything* else."

l) he went on: "I hate that son-of-a-bitch, I am going to do
   a service to the literary world, I've made up my
   mind!"

m) I asked: "you're going to expose him,
   eh?"

n) he said: "all the way."

o) well, he wrote the article.

p) and it was published in a critical
   journal.

q) and it was quite long.

r) and I read it while taking a shit.

s) then I finished it
   (the shit).

t) continued to read while taking a
   bath.

u) got out, dried off,
   went to bed.

v)   the best thing to do
w)   when a minor talent attacks a major
       talent
x)   as was the case in this
       matter
y)   is take a nap
z)   and zzzzzzzz.

shack jobs

spiders and dogs, dogs and spiders, the cross, the double-
cross, the triple-cross, spiders and dogs, I look back on the nights
and come up with very little,
remembering some of the women I lived with and realizing they
        had
nothing against me, just nothing *for* me—or for others—
those ladies
had managed to vaporize their existence, and what was
left we
shared;
dogs and spiders, the double-cross, the triple-cross and always
        the
hard carelessness for both me and for
themselves
dogs and spiders
their high-heeled shoes lonely in the corner, empty
chalices, and
as we slept our drunken sleep
I too
gave
nothing
just
my standard response: playing it
tough.
there was another better way
but it was not for us.
thusly, spiders and dogs, the double triple quadruple
cross: our hearts not willing to
love.

ground zero

the consensus is that this is a difficult time,
perhaps the most difficult of times:
large groups of people in cities
all over the world are
protesting that they'd rather not be
treated like shit.

but whoever's in control
will not listen.

the suggestion is that, of course, it's
only one power fighting another power
and the real power, of course, is in the hands
of the few who run the nations
and their need is to protect those many things
that belong to them.

it is conceivable that these few rulers
will escape
when the final eruption begins;
they will escape to their safe havens
where they will watch
the eruption to its finish,
and then after a reasonable wait
they will return
again and
will begin building
a new ridiculous and grossly
unfair future.

which, to me, is not a very
happy thought
as I crack open a can of beer
on a hot
July night.

my telephone

the telephone has not been kind of late,
of late there have been more and more calls
from people who want to come over and talk
from people who are depressed
from people who are lonely
from people who just don't know what to do
with their time;
I'm no snob, I try to help, try to suggest something that
might be of assistance
but there have been more calls
more and more calls
and what the callers don't realize is that
I too have
problems
and even when I don't
it's
necessary for me
sometimes
just to be alone and quiet and
doing nothing.
so the other day
after many days of listening to depressed and lonely people
wanting me to assuage their grief,
I was lying there
enjoying looking at the ceiling
when the phone rang
and I picked it up and said,
"listen, whatever your problem is or whatever it is you want,
I can't help you."
after a moment of silence
whoever it was hung up
and I felt like a man who had escaped.
I napped then, perhaps an hour, when the phone rang
again and I picked it up:
"whatever your problem is

I can't help you!"

"is this Mr. Chinaski?"

"yes."

"this is Helen at your dentist's
office to remind you
that you have an appointment at
3:30 tomorrow
afternoon."

I told her I'd be
there for her.

exactly right

the strays keep arriving: now we have 5
cats and they are smart, spontaneous, self-
absorbed, naturally poised and awesomely
beautiful.

one of the finest things about cats is
that when you're feeling down, very down,
if you just look at a cat at rest,
at the way they sit or lie and wait,
it's a grand lesson in persevering
and
if you watch 5 cats at once that's 5
times better.

no matter the extra demands they make
no matter the heavy sacks of food
no matter the dozens of cans of tuna
from the supermarket: it's all just fuel for their
amazing dignity and their
affirmation of a vital
life
we humans can
only envy and
admire from
afar.

3

they say that
nothing is wasted:
either that
or
it all is.

progress

this electric typer doesn't make much noise
as I continue past midnight while
the dog in the yard north barks to
the sound;
but the people there don't seem to mind
and for this I'm thankful.
from years past
I remember the room on Kingsley Ave. where
the woman downstairs would beat with a
broom handle
on the ceiling
while I typed
on my ancient manual typer
as the woman upstairs
would stamp angrily on the
floor.

those ladies were a
distraction but
I just sucked it
up
and beat the keys even
harder.

the worst one, though,
was the guy on Oxford Dr.
below me
he had a *powerful*
voice and he would
scream:
"JESUS CHRIST, KNOCK
OFF THAT FUCKING
THING!"
he would, at times,
give me pause

before I continued
but strangely enough
he never complained when
my girlfriend and I had one of
our arguments
which could be heard
half-a-block
away.

each new place I lived in
had its critics
and I was usually given a
ten p.m. curfew by
the landlord or
manager
after which
I was privileged to lay back
and listen to the babble from their
radios.

so tonight
as I listen to the barking of this
good wooly dog
next door
I am almost apologetic that I am intruding
upon his simple
life;
but bark away
little friend because,
as they say,
good literature
is almost always
disturbing.

Carter

Carter was the biggest guy in
high school, fat, aggressive
and incomprehensibly stupid;
you could *feel* the stupidity
oozing out of him and getting
into your eyes, mouth, brain.
and since they seated us
alphabetically in class and he was
Carter and I was Chinaski
I sat behind him day after day
staring at his thick round
neck
at his senseless ears and
big dumb head.
he was always raising his
hand in class,
smiling at the teacher,
making a little joke, but unfortunately
he always asked the wrong
questions.

I sat behind Carter
day after day
class after class
trying not to hate him
for his reputation
for being stupid
for being the butt
of every joke
but wishing various things
for him:
like drowning in
the bathtub or
moving to
Cedar City, Texas.

I knew in my heart, however, that he
couldn't help
what he was, he was just
a big space
where nothing grew
and that didn't make him
guilty of anything
and I knew in my heart that
because of how I felt about him
there must be something
mean and small
about me and so finally
I hung around with him
at recess
I stood up for him on the playground
and when he would turn in class and
make some dull
joke
I'd grin at him
as if we were friends
as if he had really said
something clever.

I was not always sitting behind Carter.
he was not in all my classes.

I was never a good student
but strangely
in the classes with
Carter
I got mostly "C's" and
sometimes a rare "B"
but in my other classes
I usually got a "D" and now
and then
an "F."

it got so bad that
near the end of my senior
term

a notice was sent
to my parents
that I wouldn't have
enough credits to
graduate.

my mother, a woman with
a psychotic fear of failure,
came to that school and
wept and screamed until
they told her, "all right,
Mrs. Chinaski, we'll let him
graduate."

what they meant, of course,
was that they were
getting rid
of me
and her.

during the graduation ceremony
you know who I stood behind while
waiting for my diploma.

as they called his name
he turned to me
and made a little joke
but this time
I didn't grin back
I let my expression show him
exactly
how I felt; that false
friendship must finally come
to a sad end.

and as he moved onto the stage
I
graduated.

two cats asleep downstairs and
death itself no problem

you have to wait patiently some nights
and not be embittered by the rub of Humanity.
you have to wait patiently some nights
preferably alone
not thinking about too much of anything
alone with the typer
the cigar
the electric light bulb.
you have to wait patiently some nights
for the right moment
to climb out of the trough.
there's something splendid about this ritual as
curious and easy thoughts arrive
(right now I'm remembering that the
license plate is hanging loose by one screw
from the bumper of my car).
you have to wait patiently some nights
not because of this or that or some other thing
but because it's the sensible thing to do.
you have to wait patiently some nights
not because killers prowl the streets
not because of the tax man and
not because you miss the dance of life.
suddenly I decide
right now that
tomorrow I'll add another screw to that loose license plate
because that's what keeps it and my world from falling
apart:
small desperate acts
like this enable one
to continue fighting the good fight after
waiting patiently through
the darkest night.

the pro

up in San Francisco
an editor said to me, "Hank, you bring a
suitcase when you come to read. you know,
when Diane comes to read she just carries a
little traveling bag, that's all she
needs."

well, Diane was a looker, all she needed were
some clean white panties and her miniskirt.
me, I didn't look so
good.

I said, "well, hell, I'm used to being on
the bum, I always drag a
suitcase."

"no matter," he said, "you oughta learn from
Diane, she's a pro."

I knew about Diane, she was already famous at
24, she got up and read poems about
bringing down the government and still
she got a
government grant
every year. she was beautiful, tough,
slinky and had long blonde hair down to her ass.
as she wiggled and wailed about
fascist Amerika
every man in the audience got
hot
and
some of the women
too.

and in between readings she had a

job
teaching
at a university.

now,
that editor is
dead and
Diane has vanished.
maybe she's
dead too.

I met her just
once;
fortunately
for me
we were on the same
card.
two things I liked about her:
1) at dinner before the
reading
she matched me drink for
drink
2) and her hair kept falling
into her food.

"better go easy, Diane, or I'll have to
read for both of
us."

she looked at me. "like shit," she
said, "like shit you
will."

"I can wail," I said, "and I can
wiggle. I'd love to read for you!"

"what you'd love, Chinaski," she
said, "is to fuck
me."

we both read well that night, I

think.
and that was over two decades
ago
and the government's still
here and I am
too
and
I remember Diane with special
fondness
even thought she didn't want to lay her
favors on a man almost twice her
age.

I remember
her little traveling bag
her tough talk
her humor
her perseverance
her guts
her energy
talk about a
show!

she really didn't need that
miniskirt and
change of white
panties.
they weren't necessary.

she was the real
poetry.

pain like a black-and-white snapshot

the dead dogs of yesterday (it's twilight in Missouri)
the dead dogs of nowhere (all those empty, forsaken lives)
the dead dogs of tomorrow (and the purple sun-
rise)
the dead dogs of Hades (my love with a broken
heart)
the dead dogs of our love and the dead vanilla dogs with ice
      cream
eyes (and please don't forget the shy dog in the north
yard).

dogs.

the aviator dogs the president dogs the dogs that
crawl the wallpaper and the dogs that bring an early taste of
      Novem-
ber;
the dogs that burn down the town and the dogs who
whimper and creep while promise sings like a lost
soul.

I was a young dog of 23 and you a beautiful woman
of 35
loving me burning me leaving me
my guts bleeding in the avenue while the swan
circled on the pond and watched.

now I'm an old man and you've been dead for 30 years.

and often I'm alone.

I still walk a frozen path
often getting lost and trapped and fooled again

but you were the first lovely
bitch
to take that special bite out of me
in that special
way.

Life, Death, Love, Art

he had long blonde hair
shoulder length
smoked a pipe
claimed he looked just like
Lord Byron.
he was both intellectual and handsome
and all the girls loved him
for a while.

he always had a new girl
on the string
some young fawning thing.

I knew him at a time
when things were
going very badly for me
in every possible way.
but he liked having me around.
he found something amusing
about my
suicidal and shiftless
ways.

he made a good living
poking around in the
editorial field.
he always seemed comfortable,
always in control.
he lived in an expensive
arty place with
antique furniture and
beautiful rugs
and always
some new girl
at his feet

on one of those rugs
listening
with admiration
as he spoke.

I'll admit
I tried to arouse
some interest in myself
in his girls
but they hardly ever even
glanced
in my direction.
of course,
when I would examine myself
later
in my bathroom mirror
I'd notice, say,
a shoe untied,
a couple of buttons missing
from my ragged shirt.
I'd notice my worn
shoes, yellow
teeth, facial scars,
etc.

of course,
I didn't expect
any of his girls
to go to bed with me.
I just wanted a look, a
smile,
some conversation.
but
I never got even that much.
it was as if I wasn't
in the room
at all.
and this didn't just happen
with one of his
girls,
it happened with all

of his girls.

so I began to study
him
to find out
what he had
that I lacked.

first, I saw he was very
scrubbed,
spotless.
his clothing was
fresh, clean.
his shoes
in the latest style
and brand new.
he sat relaxed
but erect
never slouching
and he didn't
gulp his drinks
he *sipped*
his drinks.

but it must have been
his conversation that
won them over.
I noticed that he
always spoke
with his beautiful accent and
with high seriousness of
Life, Death, Love, Art.
he went on
and on
never at a loss for words
talking about
Life, Death, Love, Art.

and he always referred
in his soft tones
to the same dear departed:

Shelley
Keats
Byron
Oscar Wilde
George Bernard Shaw
Chopin
George Sand
H. G. Wells
Debussy
Socrates
Santayana
and all
the other people who
didn't
interest me.

one night I decided to
get out of there and
leave him alone
with his girls.

six months or more
went by.
I was sitting
in my cheesebox room
closer to suicide than
salvation when
my landlady
knocked on the door:
"somebody wants you
on the telephone. how'd
they get
this number?"
"hell, Clara," I told
her, "I don't even know this
number."

I went down and
picked up the phone.
it was Lord Byron himself.
he was drunk.

"hey, Lord," I asked,
"how'd ya get my
number?"

"never mind ... do come
quickly ... I've been
drinking for weeks ... I
think I'm going to *kill*
myself! hurry, please!"

I got his new address
jumped into my
12-year-old car
and drove on
over.

he had evidently
moved down
from his fancy place
in the hills.
he was just off
Fountain Ave.
near the
Hollywood Police
Station.

I parked and
got out.

I found him in
a small shack
in the rear
behind a broken
screen door.
there wasn't even
a bed
in there.

he was lying on a
cot.
and he was

out cold.

I shook him:
"hey, Byron,
wake up!"

he stirred.
a lock of blond hair
fell down across his
forehead:
"oh, Henry, hello."

"got anything to
drink?" I asked.

"yes, there is some
scotch. do
pour us some ..."

I found the fifth
almost empty,
poured two drinks.

he said, "just put
mine
on the table."

I drank mine and
poured myself
another.

"Henry," he asked,
"have you ever thought of
suicide?"

"yeah."

just then
the screen door opened
and a new one
(to me)

blew in:

long
red-brown hair
long slender legs
clear
hazel eyes.

"get out of here,"
she told me.

"what do you mean?"
I asked.

"I mean, *you've* done
this
to him!
I *know* your rotten type!"

"listen, I just got
here!" I told her.

she looked down at
him: "Nelson, are you
all right?"

"Sybil," he said.

Sybil went to the cot
sat
on the edge of it
bent
over him
her long hair
falling across his face.
"Nelson, darling, are you
all right?"

I stared at
her legs
her buttocks

her breasts.

I finished my
drink.

I left.

I drove
right by the
Hollywood Police
Station

and that was
20 years
ago and

I haven't seen
either of them
since.

sometimes when you get the blues
there's a reason

it only takes 6 or 8 inept political leaders
or 8 or 10 artsy-fartsy writers, composers and painters to
set the natural course of human progress
back
50 years
or more.
which may not seem like much to you
but it's over half your lifetime
during which time you're not going to be able to
hear, see, read or feel that
necessary gift of great art which
otherwise you could have experienced.
which may not seem tragic to you
but sometimes, perhaps, when you're not feeling so
good at
night or in the morning or at
noon,
maybe what you feel that's lacking is
what *should* be there for
you
but is not.
and I don't mean a blonde in
sheer pantyhose,
I'm talking about what gnaws at your guts
even when she's
there.

the Word

they rang at 10:25 a.m.
Sunday morning.

I put on my dead father's
bathrobe with one sleeve
missing
and
opened the
door to

a woman in dark glasses and
a man.

"how are you feeling today?" he
asked.

"not well."

he shoved some religious materials
toward me.

"please. I don't want
those."

"we are all made by the same
Creator," he said.

"I am the Creator," I answered
and closed the
door.

then they walked down to the
other drunk's place in the
back and pressed his
bell.

he told them to
get the fuck away
for Christ's sake
to leave him
alone.

God's not much of a cure
for hangovers.

my nudie dancer

some years ago
I knew this nudie dancer, it was a
gentle friendship, she was one
I'd just rather look at.
yes, we did it once or twice but
she had her own life
her hobby was painting
she painted badly and she
had a series of boyfriends
all just alike:
dull fellows who wore their shirts
open
and
wore
gold neck chains
dressed sharp
and moved as if they were
walking on eggs.
they all had
little buttocks
like grapefruit halves
but they never lasted or maybe
she never
lasted.

"I can talk to you," she told
me as if that was something
marvelous.
what she meant was that I
seemed to be
listening.

I liked to watch her
nervously walking about her
apartment

lighting cigarettes
cursing
changing into different
outfits
3 or 4 times a
night.

I found her funny
she made me
laugh,
not so much laugh as
made me
smile or grin.

she was into crank,
had no luck with her
men at
all
while I was being shot down continually
by hard numbers
from the street

so

we had this little club
where we exchanged conversation about
our continuing love
failures.

about the ladies,
my complaint was mostly directed against
myself: I believed in too much
too early
and when reality
arrived I couldn't
stand it.

her complaint was almost the
opposite: "I knew the guy
was dumb ... and when a dumb
guy can't get it up

anymore then there's not
a lot left!"

"sex," I told her, "what's all this
talk about sex? is that *all* there
is?"

she said, "everything
helps."

it was the first time then
that I said it to
her: "human relationships just
never work!"

she acted as if she hadn't
heard.
she said, "you've never seen
me dance,
have you?"

"no."

"why don't you come watch me
at work
tomorrow night?"

I told her, "well, all
right."

the next night I was seated at
a table
she was standing at the bar
saw me
came on over and
sat down across from
me, she looked
good
very good.

I thought, if I let myself

I could fall in love now
and be in terrible trouble
later.

"you know," she said, "I'm
serious, I think I like you
more than any man I've known
in a long time.
I guess it's because you're not
always hitting on me.
you're *kind,*
I can feel
it."

"do you always talk like that
before you strip?"

"always," she laughed,
finishing her drink. "now I've
got to go."

she left.
there were a couple of opening
acts.
there wasn't a band
just a loudspeaker blaring
as the young girls
danced their
dismal torture
until they finally
were naked under the soft
purple lights.

it was
very discouraging
as if their essence
after all that
meant nothing at all.

some time went by
then *she* came

out.

it was different
you could see it right away
she had the body language
she knew how to move and
she
was good.

she looked all around the
club.

the barkeep waved his bar
rag

I waved a paper
napkin

and

she got into
it

dancing
shaking
clowning

singing and
laughing

then she stared
straight at me
like
never before.

her eyes were
laughing too.

you could hear the
guys in the club getting
excited

sounding
off
groaning
joking
throwing money on the
stage.

gradually,
finally, she
disrobed.

then she stood
straight, her
arms held out.

that beautiful body was
as if nailed
to a cross;
then the purple lights
went out
and she was gone behind
a curtain.

a little while later
when she came to my
table
I felt *very* special.

I ordered a couple
of drinks.

"did you like me?"
she asked.

"all the way."

"maybe we can be
better friends now?"

"I'd like that," I
told her.

we drank for maybe 15
minutes
when this fat guy
walked up.
he must have weighed 300
pounds and was well over
6 feet tall.
he stood there a
moment
then he looked down at
her.

"let's go, Isabel,"
he said.

"o.k., Daddy." she started to
pick up her
purse.

"you don't have to
go with this guy," I
told her.

"who's this jerk?" the fat
guy asked. "should I
handle him?"

"no, Tony, he's all right, don't...
please... he's an old
friend."

she looked frightened,
stood up.

"let's go, baby," said fat
boy.

I grabbed a beer bottle and
stood up.
"I'LL KICK YOUR
ASS, WHEATCAKE!"

Wheatcake snapped his fingers
and
two guys came up behind
me.

first I felt myself being lifted and
rushed through space

it was a
floating, helpless
sensation

the second thing I felt was
the unforgiving surface of a charming
cobblestone alley.

my last feeling was one of having
been fucked over, again.

I got up
went to the parking lot
found my car
got in
put the key into the
ignition
turned it on
hit the gas
it started
it
stalled

and
as I kicked it over
again the
black Cadillac came
by
just like
in a movie
fat boy driving,
Isabel
laughing and

lighting a
cigarette.

I realized then and there
that
almost anything that might
occur upon planet
earth
would have very little to do with
what I really
wanted
or
might want

so I decided not to see her
again
as if that would solve
anything at all for me
this time
the next time
or
the time after the
next.

I can't see anything

I can't see anything but
mutilated twilight.
I would like to venture forward
with hope
not only for human survival
but also for the survival of human
thought and music and art and painting and even our
history,
but you know it's like a tip I got once from
my bookie:
don't bet on it.
I see it all now
turning to burnt bacon
cripped van goghs begging pennies from
crippled bankers,
everything going like that
everyone begging and drifting
down the twisted landscape
into the valleys
the condemned
audience wailing:

    you know,
    all this
    is what we deserve.

the dark is empty;
most of our heroes have been
wrong.

not exactly the sun

it's a yellow light.
I mean walking down the street
it's a yellow light
there
soundless.

picking up the telephone
or peeling an orange
it's there
the same yellow light.

shoot an arrow through it
and it's still there
still yellow.

fight with your woman
at night
it moves across the room
stands between you
still yellow—
it's got a
head
fat arms
obese body
wide legs
no eyes.

I saw it at my mother's funeral
I saw it last night in the garden
I saw it sliding among the bottles at
the supermarket
I don't know what it is.
it sits inside of me now
and yet it looks out at me
from the walls.

we can't nail this one to the cross
we can't ask it to leave
we'll have to live with it
like we live with dresser drawers
dogs
cats
landlords.

if it comes to see you
don't try to phone me.
I'm unlisted
now.

the doomed lady poet

I met her down at the beach after a reading.
it was the morning after and
while my woman slept I got into my walking
shorts and went down the back steps and there
was the sand and the water and then I heard her
voice and went over and she introduced me
to her man—a very pretty young fellow she had just
married.
she was not a handsome woman and so much of the
good poetry she wrote was about her bad luck
with men.
"were you at the reading?" I asked her.
"no," she said, "we didn't go."
"I'm not feeling well this morning," I said.
"you have great legs," she said.
"thanks," I answered, "I've got to go now."
I walked off along the shore.

her husband—not long after—ran off with
a man and she had more angry poems to write.

the next time I saw her was in a cafe
overlooking the water. "isn't that Sandra?"
my woman asked me.
"no wonder she's been staring
at us," I replied.

I walked over to her table.
"hello," I said, "I thought it might be you."
she introduced me to the two men at her table,
horrible land creatures—long hair sticking
out all over them.

when I got back to my table I told my woman,
"let's get out of here."

I left the money and the tip for our drinks
and we drove off down the coast
looking for another place to eat.

I don't know why I'm always trying to get
away from her. I think she's too willing to
suffer. I see her sitting like a
target waiting for the slings and arrows.

we found a restaurant further south on the coast
and while we were looking at the menu
over the first drink
my woman asked me,
"are you in love with her?"

I nodded toward a waitress carrying a
Dungeness crab.

"see that crab?"
"yes."
"I'd be much happier with
it."
"and how about me?
would you be happier with me?"

the ocean was blue and green
more blue than green and there was only
one boat on it and I couldn't see
China.

"I thought we discussed that last night,"
I replied.

202

the eternal horseplayers

not much originality there:
they stand in long lines between races
making their little bets
hoping that the impossible dream
comes true for them.

not much chance:
run-down shoes,
shirt tails hanging,
they lose all day

to go back to rooming-
houses
thinking of all the plays
they could have made.

but *could have* is no good,
it has to be *now*
and they don't know
how to deal with *now*, they'll
never know while

opening an evening news-
paper
checking the next day's
entries.

thank god and the devil
hope seldom abandons any of us;
when that happens
it's cancer
or heart attack
or playing checkers with
your old lady
as she talks about
what they talk about.

first day, first job

it was high school all over again at
Union Pacific Railroad.
as I walked up the gravel path toward the foreman
they were waiting, 3 of them standing in my way.
(Jesus Christ, it never stops. the same thing
over and over again. will it
never stop?)

they waited as I walked toward the foreman,
blocking my way.

"new guy, huh?" said the smallest one as he
grinned, reached down, grabbed his lower
parts.

"what the hell's *that* supposed to mean?"
I asked.

"hey, man," said the next guy, "you looking for
trouble?"

numero uno, the leader, stood between
them with his slick black hair, his arms at
his sides, his fingers with many
rings waiting to rip your
face and eyes.
numero uno was handsome in a dumb, vicious way.
he was nearly a grown man.
he had probably already screwed a woman.
his black hair and black shoes shone in the morning
sun.

"hey, prick," he said, "fuck
off!"

I looked at him, then at the other two and
thought, well, I guess I am going to have to try to
kill them all.

I closed my eyes and
swung a right hook which caught
numero uno on the
nose. the other two backed
off. as I followed
I heard the foreman
yell: "HEY, CUT THAT SHIT
OUT!"

the leader held his hand to his
nose, crimson blossoming between his
fingers as he turned
to the foreman: "the son-of-a-
bitch hit me!"

the foreman walked over and made a
speech about how they didn't tolerate that
sort of thing at Union Pacific
Railroad. we were one big family, we were a
brotherhood and
I was lucky he didn't let me go
right then and there
but
he'd give me *one* more chance
but
any more crap *like that* and I was
finished.

"PUNCH IN!" he screamed.

we did, and were divided into different
work gangs.

nobody in my gang talked to me
which was fine.

an hour or so

later
at the water fountain
numero uno
was
standing there.

"I'm gonna get you, man!" he
hissed.

I walked back to my
work station more than
a little worried.

but
nothing happened
that day or
the next
or
in the weeks that
followed.

then
I got lucky in a crap
game, quit and took a bus
to New Orleans.

I had finally learned that
the guys who talk tough
hardly ever
are.

long sad story

Mama Norman's was just south of
downtown L.A., a little east of
Broadway, probably gone to warehouses
and parking lots now, and
I'd come downstairs in the morning and
Mama and old Jeff would be sitting
in the kitchen and she'd say,
"Hank, feed the chickens and I'll
pour you a drink," and I'd get some
feed out of the sack, put it in a pot
and go out into the cold sunshine yard
and I'd throw the yellow stuff
to the chickens like a god.
they'd come wildly to life from the
spray of my hands and then I'd
go back inside and sit down and the
bottle would be sitting there
in the soft sunlight
and old Jeff would pour, his hand like the
bark of an oak tree, telling long sad stories,
and the oven would be on,
a little gassy, and we'd sit there
with our drinks, and soon
down mine would go, good whiskey
making that kitchen as dramatic as
any play, and there I was a young man sitting
with these old people and drinking
and they treated me as an equal
by god by god
the chickens were full of grain
and old Jeff would roll a cigarette
and Mama Norman would say something,
and then one more drink all around, the
sunshine coming in like redemption
through the curtains

and then I'd go back upstairs
to my room
which was away from the sun and
smelled of centuries of damp,
but there was my port wine,
the tears of grapes, and the whore from the
south room knocking on my door
and she was naked and round
and white and terrible
as she told me about the night before,
about her men, and then about her sons,
I looked like one of them, she said,
and the cabinet radio played
and she danced all naked and fat and
white and terrible, insane really, and the only
thing to do was to get more wine, drink more
wine and wait for
morning and the chickens once
again.

the theory of the leisure class

the best thing about old women is
that all they want from you are
the simple things.

I used to feed the chickens for
my landlady, Mrs. McCarthy

and afterwards
in the breakfast nook she'd
pour me
half-a-glass of
whiskey.

we'd sit there as the morning sun came in
through the curtains.

Mrs. McCarthy asked me
once,
"you're a young man,
why don't you get a
job?"

I nodded toward the
chicken coop and
said, "I got
one."

"Lord, boy," she said,
"you're just no damned
good!"

I smiled.
unexpected praise such as that
helped
keep me
going.

divorce

maybe when I was seven or
eight
I remember the day
we decided to play
house.
we got a big blanket
took it out to
the backyard
propped it up with sticks
and we all crawled
under there.

we each had a wife.
Frank got Stella.
Gene got June.
and I got
Charlene.
Charlene had the bluest
eyes
they just burned
blue
and she was quiet
in a red dress.

I had crappy parents and
wasn't used to being close to
anybody and
we all huddled
together
under that blanket.
Charlene and I put our
arms around each
other.
we didn't kiss or anything
we just held each

other
and I had never felt
so good.
then it ended: one of
the guys got mad about
something and kicked the
blanket off.

it was Gene.
"let's get the hell our
of here," he said.

Charlene got up and
stood there
and I stood as close
to her as I could
and her blue eyes
looked right through me.
"goodbye," I said to
her as
she just looked at me with
those clear blue eyes.

for some days
I talked to Frank and
Gene about how
wonderful Charlene
was.

it was some time
later that Gene got me
off to one
side.

"listen," he said,
"don't tell anybody
but I'm going to tell you
something about
Charlene."

"what is it?"

Gene leaned real close
and whispered,
"she wears *rubber*
panties!"

"*really!*"

"really!"

after that I stayed away from
Charlene.
I mean I'd see her
out in front of her house
now and then as I
walked by.

but I wouldn't look at her.
I'd walk by as if
she wasn't there.

those blue eyes were
terrible, a god-damned
lie.

no wonder

Tony phoned and told me that
Jan had left him but that he was all right;
it helped him he said to think about other great men
like D. H. Lawrence
pissed off with life in general but still
milking his cow;
or to think about
T. Dreiser with his masses of copious
notes
painfully constructing his novels which then made
the very walls applaud;
or I think about Van Gogh, Tony continued, a madman
who continued to make great paintings as the
village children threw rocks at his
window;
or, there was Harry Crosby and his mistress
in that fancy hotel room, dying together, swallowed by
the Black Sun;
or, take Tchaikovsky, that homo, marrying a
female opera singer and then standing in a freezing
river hoping to catch pneumonia while she went mad;
or Dos Passos, after all those left-wing books,
putting on a suit and a necktie and voting Republican;
or that homo Lorca, shot dead in the road, supposedly
for his politics but really because the mayor of that
town thought his wife had the hots for the poet;
or that other homo Crane, jumping over the rail of the boat
and into the propellor because while drunk he had
promised to marry some woman;
or Dostoevsky crucified on the roulette wheel with
Christ on his mind;
or Hemingway, getting his ass kicked by Callaghan
(but Hem was correct in maintaining that F.
Scott couldn't write);
or sometimes, Tony continued, I remember that guy

with syphilis who went mad and just kept rowing in
circles on some lake—a Frenchman—anyhow, he
wrote great short stories ...

listen, I asked, you gonna be all
right?

sure, sure, he answered, just thought I'd phone, good
night.

and he hung up
and I hung up, thinking Jesus
Christ no wonder Jan left
him.

macho hell

listen, I now forgive all the women who have
lived with me and then left me
in order to find someone else to fuck,
to snort coke with, to drink with or maybe just to
talk to.

I realize now that often I am a dull
fellow and also by nature not much good at
expressing affection, and in addition
most of the time we simply weren't interested
in the same thing and/or things.

but I must tell you now that back then it was
difficult for me to forgive or under-
stand; I remember many nights of macho
hell
just looking at the walls
or an unmade bed
or yesterday's newspaper on the floor; the
minutes strangled inside my head;
and there was always female detritus scattered about:
clothes on the bed, shoes on the floor, lipstick on
the dresser, a hairbrush in the bathroom…

and then there was my precious ego, never being able
to understand how any of you could prefer
someone else to me.
there were many nights spent walking to and fro across
the room, refusing to accept, doubled over, grabbing
my gut with both hands, growling, "shit, shit,
shit…"

and trying to forget, going to cheap bars,
looking, seldom finding, and when finding playing
a role I really didn't like, just hoping for

some kind of cheap vengeance
instead of accepting what should have been accepted
gracefully.

I understand that
I never would have met any of you
if you hadn't left someone else for me or been discard-
ed by someone else—
so here's to the good nights along with all the bad:
at our best we experienced as much joy as any
one
and I thank all of you for giving me your
best;
you live in my heart and if there's a heaven
somewhere
someday you'll all be there
as
the great white shark continues to circle endlessly
in captivity
with stunned eyes, with dumb stunned
eyes.

you know who's best

it's warm here
there's a roof overhead and a radio
and some good white wine.

it's raining and I lost at the track
today.

yesterday I won $680.
today I lost $750.

Madeline
we fight and we fight.

but tomorrow I'm going to win so
pick your panties up off his
floor
and come back to
me.

he died April 9, 1553

catching the flu
and reading Rabelais.

as the cat snores,
as the toilet
down the hall
hisses,
my eyes burn.

I put Rabelais down:
this is what
writers do
to each other.

for him, I
substitute
a tab of
vitamin C.

if we could only swallow
death
like that (I think we
can).
or if death could only
swallow us
like that (I think it
does).

life is not all that
we think it
is, it's only what we
imagine it to
be and for us
what we imagine
becomes

mostly so.

I imagine myself
rid of this
flu

I see myself parading the
sidewalks along with the kings
and princes
of this world ...

meanwhile, the cat, like most other
things, pushes too
close;
I move him
gently away, thinking, Rabelais
you were a
mighty mighty interesting
fellow.

as I stretch out
to sleep
the ceiling watches me
and waits.

pick-up

the rivers the dogs won't swim,
we cross.

the women other men don't want,
we love.

the horse that wears the bandage,
we bet.

sit me down at a bar with 3 women:
one, faintly obnoxious;
one, generally stupid;
and the third,
a killer:

the killer will leave her stool
and come sit next to me.

the gods always make sure.
the gods watch over me.
they fix me up
real good.

"hi, honey," she asks, "how ya
doin'?"

"what're ya drinkin'?" I ask.

she states her drink.
I order her a drink and another for
me.

outside, it's much nicer: cars are
crashing; buildings burn;
future suicides

whistle through their teeth while
walking west or east or south or
north.

"whatcha got on your mind?" she
asks.

"I hope the Dodgers lose," I tell
her, then I
get up, go to the men's room, sneak out,
then slip through the rear
exit.

there's an alley out there.
I walk west
whistling through my
teeth.

it's all right

small cheap rooms where you walk
down the hall to the
bathroom can seem romantic to
a young writer.
even the rejection slips are
amusing because you are sure that
you are
one of the best.

but while sitting there
looking across the room
at the portable typer
waiting for you on the table
you are really
in a sense
insane

as you wait for
one more night to arrive to sit and
type Immortal Words—but now you
just sit and think about it
on your first afternoon in a strange city.

looking over at the door you
almost
expect a beautiful woman to walk in.

being young
helps get you through
many senseless and terrible
days.

being old
does
too.

one of those crazy nights

we were sitting at a table; I'd known him when he'd
lived in Munich working at something that we were mutually
interested in; now he'd come down from Montana, still working
    at
something that we were both more or less mutually interested
in.
we'd been in a bar maybe 3 or 4 hours. he had a nose like the
beak of a hawk and he was 6-foot-4 and wore a dumb cowboy
hat.
we were drinking scotch with beer chasers when he leaned
forward (it was a crowded Saturday night) and whispered: "you
    take
the guys at the bar and I'll take the guys at the other table; we'll
    clean
this place out, o.k.?"
I narrowed my eyes, looked around: "no, you take the guys at the
    bar and I'll take the guys at the other table."
"o.k.," he said, "now?"
"wait," I said, "let's have another drink
first."
"o.k.," he said, "I wanna see the waitress again anyway. did you
    see her
boobs?"
"yeah."
"man, what TITS!"

I motioned the girl over for another round; she came with her
loaded tray.
it happened fast: he reached up and grabbed one of her
breasts.
such a god-damned SCREAM you never heard along with the
    crash of a dropped
tray
and then it looked like the whole bar was coming after us!

"FOLLOW ME, COWBOY!" I yelled
and I ran up the stairway to the crappers.
just to the west of the crappers there was a window
where the slanted roof almost reached the ground.
I climbed out onto the roof with the cowboy just behind and then
we jumped and hit the good earth and really started running.
we leaped over a vine-covered fence into a yard where a huge dog
     with red
eyes barked with great *verve*. one of us kicked him in the balls
     and
then we were out of there and
found ourselves walking along a quiet tree-lined street with
     nobody
about.

I had sprained my right ankle, each step I took was fire from
hell and the cowboy said, "we ought to go back there and kick
     some
ass!"

"you really think we should?"

"why not?"

"I can give you many good reasons," I said.

"you're right," he said, "let's go back to your place."

"sure," I said, "but one more
thing..."

"what's that?"

"first we gotta find the fucking
car."

and with that we moved forward into the night, once again joined
     by a
mutual interest.

urban war

the black car and the yellow truck
crashed violently in
the center of the intersection.
the black car was stopped in its tracks
and sat there honking
while the yellow truck veered off from the
collision
and came directly toward me
sideways
with the driver slumped over the wheel.
I should put my car in reverse,
I thought, but my hand couldn't find
the gear shift quickly enough.
then the yellow truck began to skip off
to one side
and I thought, it's not going to hit
me directly, it's going to scrape my
door and then it passed by on the right,
silently,
you couldn't have slipped a sheet of paper
between us.
then the yellow truck crashed head-on into the
car of a man stopped to my right two
car lengths back.
the yellow truck drove him into a third car, bounced off,
slanted across the
street, ran up over a curb and was still.

I had not seen the initial crash
I had only heard it.
I drove over into a gas station
turned off the engine
and sat there
looking at the four crashed cars.
there was not a sound.

if I had been able to put it into reverse,
I would be sitting over there
with them now.
I started the engine and drove
out, thinking, let's see. where was I
going? oh yes, the post office.
I needed stamps.

good pay

I went to this same college to read again
after many years
and the same professor was there
in his office
opening his desk drawer
to hand me another fat cigar
as my new girlfriend stood and watched.

and
after a while we three walked outside
and
the campus was high on a hill
all very green
and
all the young girls were strolling by
just as they had strolled by
many years ago
and
I told him, "it's strange, the girls
don't get old here."
"think nothing of it," he told me

an hour or so later I read
got my check
and then we all went back to the prof's place
for a few drinks.

he had a new wife (a
recent student); the prof was making
out, feeding upon the eternal youth
of the campus.

I reached under his wife's dress and
patted a hunk of flank.
then I turned to the prof who was

bringing us whiskey sours.
"how do you get a job like yours?"
I asked him.

he passed the drinks out, laughed and
sat down.

"I was going to ask you the same thing,"
he said.

then I noticed my young girlfriend
pressed up against an English major
and giggling.

"it's easy," I said, "all I do is
lie as truthfully as possible."

"that's the best description of poetry
I've heard in a long time," he replied.

I watched my girlfriend flirting with the
English major.

"don't worry about that kid," said
the prof.

"how come?"

"no originality. you're his main literary
influence."

we finished our drinks.

"you make a great whiskey sour," I told
him. "how about another?"

"sure," he said, got up and left.

I reached up under his wife's dress and
grabbed some more flank.

she yanked my hand away:
"do that one more time and I'll kick you in your
balls!"

then my girlfriend came over with the
English major.

"this is Sonny Sanderson," she said,
"he wants to meet you."

I stood up and we shook hands.

"Sonny and I are going to the dance tonight!" said
my girlfriend. "he says he's a good
dancer."

"you can really write," he said. "how
do you do it?"

"thanks," I said, "but we've got to leave
now. it's a long drive back to L.A."

so after finishing the whiskey sour I got up
and my girl came along as Sonny Sanderson loomed large
in the professor's doorway.
we got into the car
and
on the drive back I knew how I was going to hear all
about it: how I was no good at parties, how I was
afraid of people and that I couldn't enjoy myself
and how I often imagined things that weren't true
and even though I acted very superior
I was actually a very insecure person.

all of which was probably true.

she kept switching stations on the car radio
and she kept plugging in the dashboard lighter
to re-light her cigarette which kept going out
and as her hair kept falling down into her
face

I checked my coat pocket to see of the reading
check was still there.
I turned into the freeway entrance
glided into the fast lane
turned on the wipers to clear the fogged-up
windshield
and waited to hear all about
it.

panasonic

I haven't killed all the spiders in this place
but I've gotten most of them. there are two
I can't get. they sit inside the plastic shield
on my radio, solid-state FM-AM, they sit
inside where the red dot selects the station.
I only listen to FM on two Los Angeles
stations, KUSC and KFAC, in that order. they are
both classical music stations.

those are newly cultured spiders. they heard Beethoven's
9th last night and now they are listening to Brahms'
2nd. what they are feeding on I am not sure, but
they seem satisfied. only their legs move
now and then.

that radio is educating them. they are now starting
to look like some critics I know. by this, please
understand that I mean no offense to the spiders.

out of place

I always knew that there was something wrong
with me.
it got worse in Jr. High School.
when I walked into a room
all the students would begin talking
at once
it got very noisy
and I would stand and stare at them
and they would talk louder and louder
until the teacher would bang on the
desk:
"ALL RIGHT! ALL RIGHT! THAT'S ENOUGH
OF THAT!"

I had no idea of what excited them
and as I sat at my desk
heads would often turn and
stare at me.

these occurrences were commonplace
and because I never did anything untoward or
unusual
I just knew that there must be something
wrong with me.

the teachers, too, acted strangely:
"WHAT ARE YOU DOING, MR. CHINASKI?"
(I wouldn't be doing anything)
"YOU WILL PLEASE REMAIN AFTER CLASS!"

it was usually the female teachers
who acted like this
and I liked all my female teachers
even though I felt sorry for them and
afterward they never explained to me

what I had done wrong
and I never asked.

on the school grounds it was also
strange:
girls and boys I didn't know would walk up
to me and
ask, "how are you doing, Henry?"
and for some odd reason I'd always reply,
"get away from me!"

what it all meant,
I never knew.
I had no plans, few desires and
no impulses.
I sensed that there was something
really wrong and
that I was a freak.

but since it felt neither good nor
bad,
I accepted the situation and
waited.

a great place, here

sitting here with my pal
Kraft Meyerbeer
we saw the wetbacks climbing over the wall.
Kraft zonkered the first one with a fireball
I got the second with my old luger
and then Kraft
he got the third one
who looked a little bit like Marlon Brando
he got him in the ass with his
crossbow.
New Mexico is a great place to be,
down here by the border.
Kraft and me
we sit in the back yard all day
under the shade trees
listening to Brahms and John Cage
and drinking peppermint tea laced with
gin.
sometimes at night the whores come
floating over the wall with their
big pink balloon breasts
and we slingshot them down with
razor rocks of
quartz.
they scream,
piss, flop in the
cacti.
or sometimes we'll catch a wild dog and
skin him alive.
things get better and better.
yesterday we killed a cop, stuck his balls
in his mouth
and left him on a park bench in the town
plaza.
on Sundays we either burn churches or

make our own
ice cream.
the other day a guy put a dent in my fender
so I chained him to my front bumper
and drove all the way to
Phoenix
like that
and when I got there I rammed him
to shit
against the fanciest whorehouse in town.
nobody much bothers us out here,
although they've threatened to call out
the state troopers.
now we don't want to hurt those
nice boys,
lots of them have mothers and sisters
and sweethearts
so I hope they stay away.
you ought to see our garden
best garden in town
best in the world
like the Garden of Eden
except no snake would dare enter
here.

well, thanks for listening
come on down and visit me
anytime ...
we'll find you
something interesting
to do.

horses don't bet on people and neither do I ...

I look for a seat alone but a couple of rows in
front of me sits a bald old man in a grey
sweater.
he has a voice you can hear for 40 yards.
the year is 1980, he is talking about some
horse that won a stakes race in 1958.
he had bet him to win.
"HE WAS 13-TO-ONE! THE HORSE HAD NEVER RUN
MORE THAN SEVEN FURLONGS AND THEY WERE ENTERING
HIM IN A MILE-AND-ONE-EIGHTH! WELL, SIR, HE
JUMPED IN FRONT AND WENT ALL THE WAY, THE OTHER
HORSES NEVER GOT CLOSE TO HIM! IT WAS SOME RACE!"

the man he is talking to turns his head away
and pales, he is suddenly sick.
I get up and move, I find a new seat,
the closest person to me is three seats away
and she doesn't even have a *Racing Form,* she's
working a crossword puzzle.
she looks up at me: "hey, what's a four-letter
word for 'departed'?"
"dead?"
"no, that don't fit ..."
"gone?"
"ah ... yeah, that's it. say, didn't I see you
in some movie? aren't you a movie star?"
"no."
"yes, it was a horror movie, you played a man
who fell out of a bell tower!"

I get up and walk to the escalator and
ride it down and find a bench in the sun. I sit down there
and then I find I've lost my program so I go to one of the
vendors and buy a new program.

"buying another program, buddy?" he asks.

"yeah. you remember me, eh?"

"oh yeah! I remember you!"

I walk quickly back to the escalator, pulling my hat
down over my eyes.
as I ride the escalator up, the man next to me is
carrying a portable radio and he has it turned on as
loud as it can go.

somebody is singing on that radio.
it's Barry Manilow.

my failure

I think of devils in hell
and stare at a
beautiful vase of
flowers
as the woman in my bedroom
angrily switches the light
on and off.
we have had a very bad
argument
and I sit in here smoking
cigarettes from
India
as on the radio an
opera singer's prayers are
not in my
language.
outside, the window to
my left reveals the night
lights of the
city and I only wish
I had the courage to
break through this simple horror
and make things well
again
but my petty anger
prevents
me.

I realize hell is only what we
create,
smoking these cigarettes,
waiting here,
wondering here,
while in the other room
she continues to

sit and
switch the light
on and off,
on and
off.

in memory of a dead jock

he was looking
down
trying to soothe the horse
when it reared up,
and the top of the gate
sliced behind and under the
protective helmet
of the jock
and crushed his skull.

I had a ticket on the horse,
#9. they took it back to
the barn and drove off
in an ambulance with
the jock.
some minutes later the track
announcer told the crowd
that the jock was
dead.
but the people went right on
betting.
one thing I remember, though,
is that
ten minutes after the
announcement
I saw a man jam an
entire hot dog into his
mouth, you could see the
mustard, the bun, the relish,
the dog all going in,
and then he closed his mouth on it
all
and chewed,
blinking
gulping.

he was still alive
the man with the hot dog
as the hyenas circled
and the toteboard
flashed.

repeat

it's an
old poem:
sitting here
again
at 3 a.m.
having typed a
few,
all the cigarettes
smoked,
the many pages
on the
floor,
down to
the last
glass of
wine.

now to move
the body
to the
bed

thinking,
such easy
luck, I'll
take
it:

wine and
poems.

this is the
way
the ancient
Chinese

poets
were able to
laugh at
and endure
death and
life

for their
own
sake

and for
ours.

now you know why we kiss the wall

the sermon's good
and the hot tea
spills into the falcon's
eyes.
Griff said he'd bring
the stuff at noon and
it's 1:30
already.
you know how it is:
if you found a man or
a woman you could trust
you'd doubt them for some
other reason.
Andre writes that he's
teaching acting at the
University of Illinois
and the baby I saw that
night
so long ago
over red wine and a great
Italian meal
has grown into a
golden green creature
rising into girlhood.
in this neighborhood now
the other older girls keep
coming by
at midnight and
behind the barns
the cats sleep
in the snow.
we touch things
in our dreams
vital disturbing things
as our shoes sit under

the bed, one straight up
the other on its
side.
and I wonder why
so many great
composers have been unable to
finish more than
9 symphonies as
I get up and
walk across space
in my attempt
to find the
door.

that's who sent them

dead flowers in a vase looking across at me in a room
dark because I do not choose light; they have shut off
the water again and are now banging on the pipes; this is
a madhouse, they raided here last night and I would not
let them in, the chain held and I moved the sofa against
the door and I called my lawyer and my fat whore cried
and at last they went away; this Sunday drags its snake-
shape in and out of the light sockets, the phone rings and leaps
on the couch like a punched dog, and right away I think I may
have been poisoned as I walk over to the flowers
but my hands are too weak to take them out not now
so white white or so pink pink but rotten dead dead dead
and the squawk of a jay rips through the window like
cannonfire from an earlier age, and I stand with
dead flowers and ringing, sunlight now burning my
pale face and pale heart, and I take the
flowers white not so white, pink not so pink, it's
like turning out the light, and I throw them throw them
throw them out   OUT   as I move and answer the
phone and a voice says HAPPY BIRTHDAY DARLING.

it's just me

I am such an unpopular human
being.
I should have been born a frog,
or perhaps something a bit higher
up the trunk of a birch tree:
a red-headed woodpecker?
a bushy-tailed squirrel?

I don't seem to fit in anywhere.
in cafes, restaurants,
I say strange things to the
waiters and waitresses,
nothing ugly,
just rather airy
and not quite
befitting.
I find it funny
but nobody else does
especially
the lady with me:
"you embarrass me in
public!"

on freeways I also seem
out of place.
I slow down to allow people
who are changing lanes
to move into the space in front
of me.

I did this once
while driving with a
young lady.
she exploded in
scornful laughter:

"you don't HAVE to do
that!"

I am often at a loss
when confronted by a crisis.
once an old man
next to me
on the sidewalk
tripped and fell.
I only stared down at
him.
others rushed up
to help
(I never seem to be in
sync with the rest of
humanity)
but my first reaction had been
to think that
if I was that old man
I wouldn't want anybody touching
me
or trying to help
me.

I should have been born a rogue elephant
or a giant lizard scorched by the sun.
for example,
a friend will point a woman out
to me
and say,
"God, isn't she beautiful!"
and I will look at that face
and see a determination
a threat
so great
that I wonder why the gods
do not place a warning sign on her
that says
"LOOK OUT FOR THIS ONE
UNLESS YOU WISH TO DIE A LINGERING
DEATH."

I guess I am just out of step
with most others.
for instance, I don't sleep
like most
at regular hours.
this has given me much trouble in my
relationships.
suddenly, say at 3 p.m.,
on any afternoon
I might disrobe
climb into bed and
announce,
"I'm going to sleep now."
I do this because I feel
like sleeping then
and like to believe that
I have a right to this animal
freedom.
yet some of the ladies I have known
have found this
inconvenient
selfish
and have finally left
me
because of that
(but they would have left me
for some other reason
anyhow,
or if not,
I would have left
them).

it's a sad fact but
I disagree with almost everyone I know.
I think most movies are terrible
and television is even worse.
there is nothing I hate more than idle
conversation.
the exploration of Space
bores me

and I can find more of interest
in the daily newspaper than in
all the literature of
all the centuries.

happy to be alone
I sit here at 3 a.m. and
clip my toenails as
I think about
my favorite philosopher
who said:
"I am Popeye the Sailor Man
I live in a garbage can
I like to go swimmin'
with bow-legged wimmin
and I *yam* what I *yam*
what I *yam!*"

put that in your smoke and
pipe it.

then I know why

when I see those cowboys driving the freeways
in their bright red pickup trucks
say
on a sunny day in March
with a beautiful dog
(or dogs)
untethered and lurching in the
truck beds
I wonder about those cowboys, about
what philosophy they live with and
by,
about what noble sentiments
motivate them,
and when I pull alongside to
get a look
first at the frightened animals
and then at their heedless masters,
I am never ready
for the swell of
anger
that rises within me,
a spiritual despair
so great that
I can feel it
as something
physical,
like a hammer blow
to the gut, the head and the
mind, and
then I know why
I've had so much trouble
in the factories
in the bars
at parties
picnics

at any gathering of the
clan,
large or small:
all there is to them are
arms, legs, heads, ears, eyes, empty
parts
stitched together
without
anything meaningful inside.
there is absolutely nothing one can
say to them and
to rail against them would be
akin to
firing bullets into a pile of
shit.

the crushed animals I see
left along the side
of the freeway
both dead and dying—
we wouldn't leave humans there
like that
to expire and rot in the sun,
it would remind us
too much
of our own feeble deaths to come
which
most often
in funeral aftermath
are far
more farcical than
profound.

her only son

to endure is only
meaningful
if you come out
with
something
at the other
end.
but to endure
simply in order to
endure
is the unfortunate
plight
of millions.

I remember
the time
I buried my
love
and driving back
after the
funeral with
her only son
instead of recognizing
the fact
of his mother's
neglected and lonely
adult life and death
all
he talked about
was how much
money
he was
making
now.

he thought
he had endured
but
he
hadn't.
there was
nothing
left of
his life
to
lose.

he was like a
slab of
meat
in a
butcher shop.

and to think
she used to
talk about
him lovingly
almost
every night
before we
fell
asleep.

the wrong way

luxury ocean liners
crossing the water
full of the indolent
and rich
passing from this place to that
with their hearts gone
and their guts empty
like Xmas turkeys
the great blue sky above
wasted
all that water
wasted
all those
fingers, heads, toes, buttocks,
eyes, ears, legs, feet
asleep in
their American Express Card
staterooms.

it's like a floating tomb
going nowhere.

these are the floating dead.

yet the dead are not ugly
but the near-dead surely
are
most
surely are.

when do they laugh?
what do they think about
love?

what are they

doing
midst all that water?
and where do they seek
to go?

4

you begin by starving in cheap
rooms
and you end up by
asking your lawyer
to keep an eye on your
tax accountant.

make a poem out of
that.

I move to the city of San Pedro

when I first moved here
the neighbors were friendly.
the old couple next door
came to the fence
and she said:
"anything we can do for
you, let us know. we're
home all the time."
"thank you," I told
them.

the young couple to
the west
didn't say much.
"we keep a low profile,"
the husband told me.
"I like that,"
I said.

things were quiet for
a couple of weeks.
I dug around in the garden,
planted some corn
and radishes.

then one night
my lady and I
had a bad night.
we drank too much and
she declared
her independence
and revealed
her true feelings
about me
but either she

came on too strong
or she worded it
badly;
her tone seemed to
drip with a
pure and bitter
hatred.

anyhow,
it maddened my thought
processes
and we ended up
at 8:30 a.m. on a
very sunny Sunday morning
me naked
totally imbecilic
chasing her
through the garden while
hurling rocks
wildly and
screaming:
YOU GOD-DAMNED ROTTEN WHORE!"
and so forth and so on.

after a time, of course,
it all abated
and things became
quiet again.

now
the old couple next
door
speak to me very
little.
he, curtly.
she, never.

but the young couple
to the west
have become
friendlier.

he started coming by,
knocking, and leaving me
loaves of fresh-baked bread
from their oven.

then he came
to my New Year's party with
his wife.

as the months went on
he came over for
many beers.

recently he came
to the door with
a couple of bottles of
wine and said, "I'd like to talk
and drink with you."

then his wife arrived and
we were joined by
my lady and
we drank his two bottles.

I have never *quite* repeated
my opening act of
naked-in-the-yard-at-
8:30 a.m.

and I hope I never do

but it's curious
what
appeals to some people.

it could be that
what we think is
correct often
is
not very interesting.

sometimes I even think I'd like
to have
a neighbor
just like me

but when I really
think it through
I know that
I could not stand
that.

be angry at San Pedro

I say to my woman, "Jeffers was
a great poet. think of a title
like *Be Angry at the Sun.* don't you
realize how great that is?"

"you like that negative stuff," she
says.

"positively," I agree, finishing my
drink and pouring another.
"in one of Jeffers' poems, not the sun poem,
this woman fucks a stallion because her
husband is such a gross spirit. and it's
believable. then the husband goes out
to kill the stallion and the stallion
kills him."

"I never heard of Jeffers," she
says.

"you never heard of Big Sur? Jeffers
made Big Sur famous just like D. H. Lawrence
made Taos famous. when a
great writer writes about where he
lives the mob comes in and takes
over."

"well, you write about San Pedro," she
says.

"yeah," I say, "and have you read the
papers lately? they are going to construct
a marina here, one of the largest in the
world, millions and billions of dollars,
there is going to be a huge shopping

center, yachts and condominiums every-
where!"

"and to think," my woman says smiling, "that you've
          only
lived here for three years!"

"I still think," I say,
changing the subject,
"you ought to read Jeffers."

lost in San Pedro

no way back to Barcelona.
the green soldiers have invaded the tombs.
madmen rule Spain
and during a heat wave in 1952 I buried my last concubine.

no way back to the Rock of Gibraltar.
the bones of the hands of my mother are so still.

stay still now, mother
stay still.

the horse tossed the jock
the horse fell
then got up
on only 3 legs—
the 4th bent nearly in two
and all the people anguished for the jock
but my heart ached for the horse
the horse
the horse
it was terrible
it was truly terrible.

I sometimes think about one or the other of my women.
I wonder what we were hoping for when we lived together
our minds shattered like the 4th leg of that horse.

remember when women wore dresses and high heels?
remember whenever a car door opened all the men turned to look?
it was a beautiful time and I'm glad I was there to see it.

no way back to Barcelona.

the world is less than a fishbone.

this place roars with the need for mercy.

there is this fat gold watch sitting here on my desk
sent to me by a German cop.
I wrote him a nice letter thanking him for it
but the police have killed more of my life than the crooks.

nothing to do but wait for the pulling of the shade.
I pull the shade.

my 3 male cats have had their balls clipped.
now they sit and look at me with eyes emptied
of all but killing.

justice

you take the train from
Germany to Paris
and you know when you've
crossed the border:
the train stops and
French soldiers jump
on.
two of them run into
our compartment.
they seem angry as
we flash our passports
but they are
more interested in the
black American soldier
sitting
across from us.
they speak to him
rapidly in French.
one of them grabs him
by the coat
while the other
rips down his suitcase
from overhead
opens it
dumps the contents
on the floor.

they they
pull
the American soldier
up on his feet
indicate
for him to
put his things
back

into his suitcase
which
he does
then they yank him
out of the compartment
and
take him away.

the train sits a
while
then jerks
into motion.
soon we are at
full speed.

"that was terrible,"
says my wife,
"I wonder what he
did?"

"he was looking
up
your legs,"
I tell her.

"that's nonsense,"
she says.

"I like the French,"
I say
opening up
two miniature bottles of
red wine
for us
as the little villages in
the landscape
slip by.

a boor

we are sitting in the cafe
waiting.
I've read yesterday's race results
and today's entries over and
over.

"everybody else has rolls,"
she says. "I wonder why
our waitress hasn't brought
us our rolls?"

"which waitress is ours?"
I ask.

"you ordered. don't you
look at people?"

"not before eating. which
one is she?"

"she's over there folding
napkins. she won't look
up."

"that one?"

"that one."

I spear a napkin on my fork and
whirl it around and around
over my head.

"oh, stop that!" my woman says.

the waitress sees me and walks
over.

"where are our rolls?" I
ask.

"rolls are 75 cents
extra," she says.

"good. bring us four orders of
rolls, please."

our waitress leaves.

"besides that," my woman says, "she
hasn't brought us our order.
it's been sitting there for 5
minutes."

"how do you know?"

"I can see it sitting over there."

"I can't see anything."

"it's behind the glass partition.
I can see it."

our waitress comes with four
orders of rolls and butter.

"thank you," I say, "but I wonder
why you don't bring us our dinner?
it's been ready for 5 minutes."

"that's not your order, sir. those
are display meals."

our waitress walks off.

"eat your rolls," I say to
my lady.

"no, I don't want to spoil my
dinner."

"please pass me the front page."

"no, I'm reading it."

so I stare at a strange woman
until she turns and glares at
me.

then our order comes
only
another waitress brings
it.

"thank you," I say.

the new waitress walks off.

"the other waitress couldn't
stand you," says my lady.

"I hate to ruin somebody's
day," I say.

"well, you have."

"it happens almost everywhere
I go," I reply.

it's a good place.
they serve only seafood and the tables are
clean and comfortable.

I eat the dinner.
my woman eats hers.

I tip 15% and we leave.

walking toward our car in the parking
lot
she says, "you ate all the rolls."

"yeah," I say.

out of the dark

the tiger killed 4 wild dogs before the
rest of the pack
finished him off,
then the
rains came and the dogs shivered in the wash of water
while devouring the
tiger as at dawn today a man entered the freeway the wrong way
crashed into 7 cars
killing one commuter
injuring
eleven
as this morning for breakfast I had 4 hard-boiled eggs sprinkled
with chili powder
along with
a glass of orange
juice
while thinking about
the old man next door who died last night: I will miss watching
him tug at the crabgrass in his lawn.

the constant is in the occurring and the occurring is
constant.

beautiful things can be terrible and terrible things can be
beautiful.

I must remember
to thank the
gods later
today for all
that.

for the foxes

don't feel sorry for me.
I am a competent,
satisfied human being.

be sorry for the others
who
fidget
complain

who
constantly
rearrange their
lives
like
furniture.

juggling mates
and
attitudes

their
confusion is
constant

and it will
touch
whoever they
deal with.

beware of them:
one of their
key words is
"love."

and beware those who

274

only take
instructions from their
God

for they have
failed completely to
live their own
lives.

don't feel sorry for me
because I am alone

for even
at the most terrible
moments
humor
is my
companion.

I am a dog walking
backwards

I am a broken
banjo

I am a telephone wire
strung up in
Toledo, Ohio

I am a man
eating a meal
this night
in the month of
September.

put your sympathy
aside.
they say
water held up
Christ:
to come

**through
you better be
nearly as
lucky.**

poem for Brigitte Bardot

coronets alive with the fire of wine,
contents of flax, names, speeches,
and I see where Brigitte Bardot
cut her wrist and took some pills,
but like the rest of us she will manage to continue
in spite of everything,
and then for no reason at all I remember
another young woman
looking down from the window
in her dirty underwear
many years ago
screaming my hangover name on a
Philadelphia Sunday morning,
and I remember
the way we decorated the trees in the snow
outside the bar there
on the sidewalk
that Christmas Day
falling down like drunken bears
laughing and tramping over the tinsel.
yes, I am sorry, Brigitte, if it is not going well
for you, but it's bad all around;
you see, I have figured out that seagulls
are mad angels
trying to tell us something,
and as they dip and screech before our eyes
the sea comes up for air and spirits them
away.
so I am truly sorry, Brigitte,
that you are not doing well but
I have just turned both my pockets out
and found just three pennies
on my dresser, undress,
shave and go to sleep
although there is something wrong

with my left arm, it's stiff as hell and hurts
(polio? bad blood or something?)
and today as I walked through the supermarket
I looked at oranges and apples and cucumbers
and at the barbecued chickens turning on their spits
like great men burning in their own fire,
but since I am no thief I bought cigarettes and left,
and I still had three cents remaining
and I stood and read the headline in the paper
and saw your picture
and I looked around
and on the tall building across the street
a man crouched
ready to leap, and a dog went by with a bone
in his mouth, something dead,
and I am sorry for you, Brigitte, and I too have
love problems, but I still have my typewriter,
a radio, and all the water I can drink,
so I will have one for you, a tall
one, and I'll shake my arm, turn on the radio
and hope for Brahms or Beethoven,
and maybe in the morning the man will have
jumped, maybe I will have jumped,
and maybe through picture postcards and
coffins, through arcades of roses and screaming,
maybe through the towers and tables and Christmas trees
your lover will come and kiss you once again
under the cigarette and cucumber sun.

having the flu and
with nothing else to do

I read a book about John Dos Passos and according to
the book once radical-communist
John ended up in the Hollywood Hills living off investments
and reading the
Wall Street Journal.

this seems to happen all too often.

what hardly ever happens is
a man going from being a young conservative to becoming an
old wild-ass radical.

however:
young conservatives always seem to become old
conservatives.
it's a kind of lifelong mental vapor-lock.

but when a young radical ends up an
old radical
the critics
and the conservatives
treat him as if he escaped from a mental
institution.

such is our politics and you can have it
all.

keep it.

sail it up your
ass.

a time to remember

at North Avenue 21 drunk tank you slept on the floor and at
    night
there was always some guy who would step on your face on his
way to the crapper
and then you would curse him good, set him straight, so that
he would know enough to either be more careful or to
just lay there and hold it.

there was a large hill in back dense with foliage
you could see it through the barred window
and a few of the guys after being released would not go back to
skid row, they'd just walk up into that green hill where
they lived like animals.
part of it was a campground and some lived out of the
trash cans while others trekked back to skid row for meals but
    then
returned
and they all sold their blood each week for
wine.

there must have been 18 or 20 of them up there and
they were more or less just as happy as corporate lawyers
stockbrokers or airline
pilots.

civilization is divided into parts, like an orange, and when you
peel the skin off, pull the sections apart, chew it, the
final result is a mouthful of pale pulp which you can either
swallow or spit
out.

some just swallow it
like the guys down at North Avenue
21.

"I demand a little respect"

the strangest thing
after living with a
woman
for some
years

is that
no matter what
miraculous
things you might
accomplish

they leave
her
unimpressed.

for instance
you could leap
60 feet
straight up into
the air
and

she would
hardly
notice.

but let
somebody else
jump two inches
off
the ground and

this same woman
would

applaud
enthusiastically
as if that
was something really
special.

at times
at this bitterest
moment
one realizes that
no matter how many
years
one has lived with
the same
woman

one has really
always
lived
alone.

pink silks

I think of
new roses, angry cats, leaning fences and old
photographs of young Charles
Lindbergh
and his
Spirit of St. Louis
as *my* spirit
drives along the sea
over grumpy dirt roads
nastier than a
cheap cigar
and as I drive along
alone and carefree
the homes of the rich
up above
seem demented, unclear and
frightened
on their flattened
mountain
tops.
where *I* live now
friends turn cold and
suddenly old
and when they laugh I see their
false teeth
but at least they
laugh—
that's as important as clean
laundry.
and, over in Andernach,
my Uncle Hein
died at 93, and
I'm sure his back is as straight in the
casket as it was in
life, a stout Kraut,

my Uncle Heinrich!
the perfect music of a natural event is
astonishing:
as I watch a jockey
walking from the stable area
alone
in the finest pink silks
(with thin green
piping)
carrying his whip loosely
on his way to a waiting groom,
I see centuries of mankind
approaching the impossible
with casual courage;
the bite of reality doesn't kill,
it only clears the mind.
what I like best, I guess, is that
everything eventually
resolves itself
adjusts itself
heals itself
no matter what I think or
do, but
still, the swift and ugly course
of common and uncommon
experience
often bedazzles even those
much smarter than
myself.
so just wind me up
run me over the edge of
the coffee table to
where the sky drops into the sea—
to the last
unutterable end that one day
we all will experience and
finally know.

milk a cow and you get milk

I've mostly stopped worshipping
other writers now
past or present
but I was a writer junkie for
a long time.
I think I read every
book about D. H.
Lawrence, and those great
photos:
there was D. H.
actually milking a
cow.
and there was
Frieda and there was A.
Huxley
and all
the others.

I once thought
writing was magic
something that
magic people
did.
I didn't think it would
be like this.

I thought it would be
natural
simple
like
making toast or
skiing down a
hill.
it all looked so fucking
easy from that
distance.

oh, to be young in 1942!

4-F in Louisiana, couldn't convince the army shrink I was sane,
      didn't mind,
liked to drink but that was about all, the only talent I had—
      otherwise,
I couldn't figure out the top from the bottom from the middle—
      sitting there in the
Gang Plank Bar with toothless whores and the other idiots
of the night, the drinks were cheap but watered and I wanted to
be in love with a millionairess and live with her in a New York
      City
penthouse with green plants surrounding us with their octopus
      arms but
no, of course, it wasn't going to be that way, everything was going
      to be
dry and dumb and listless, and there I sat in my body with all
my wretched parts, right smack in the middle of American
      history which wanted
nothing to do with me and I didn't want much to do with it
      either and
it was all very strange but not too strange because my father had
      always
told me that the way I THOUGHT meant that there was no
      chance for me, that I would
always be a useless misfit doomed to early destruction and
      shame, and
I had no DRIVE, he said, and he was right because I felt best
when I was sucking on those watered drinks—
that seemed the apex of life to me—and the proudest
      accomplishment that I
could point to was my rented room across the street (paid up
for ONE FULL WEEK) that was plenty of miracle for me, and
the people in the bar thought I was crazy just like the army
shrink thought I was, and they didn't speak to me, but then they
hardly spoke to each other either
and

286

one night I got tired of the bar and I walked out and kept
walking and I walked and walked all the way down to the Gulf of
Mexico and sat there with my legs dangling over the pier
considering nothing but the waiting
and I sucked on the bottle of wine I had purchased on the way
and I listened to the water making sounds like
woosh woosh woosh
over and over again
and I liked that but the water stank and I got up and
walked around the edge of the pier and into the profound
    darkness
and I was drunker than usual and then I was walking
through deep mud with a light rain falling and I thought, man,
    you
must be crazy like they say
or
why would you keep walking through this mud?
and then a searchlight was shined on me from a tower
(I saw the tower framed behind the light and I thought, what the
    hell
is that?) and a voice screamed "HALT!"
the war was everywhere and I had stumbled into forbidden
territory and I turned and started running and the
LIGHT FOLLOWED ME. then there
was a shot and then another shot (and a pause) and then another
shot. somebody was
firing at *me* but
why? and I stumbled and fell headlong into the mud
then
I got up and I thought, fuck it, this fits my suicide wish
perfectly
and I stopped running
I walked away and
there were a couple more shots but not nearly as close as
the others and I kept walking through the mud until I found a
street and I walked up the street and
I walked all the way back to the *Gang Plank Bar*
and I walked in and sat down and ordered a drink. I
was covered with mud—all over my face, hands, clothing—yet
nobody said anything and the bartender served me and I picked
    up

my watered drink and drank it down
ordered another
drank it down
and then just for the hell of it I
didn't pay I
just walked out of there and back to my room
        sat in a corner like Little Jack Horner

took off my shoes
my stockings
all heavy with mud
and I thought, I'm never going back to that bar again
and I didn't
(it was the most depressing place I had ever
been and I had been in
plenty like it)
so
too drunk to undress and not wanting to dirty the
roominghouse sheets
I slept on the floor
to be checked out later
by my roomies
the roaches
for sanity or whatever it was they were
looking for.

the condition book

the long days at the track have
swallowed and consumed
me.
I am the horses, the jocks, I am six furlongs, seven
furlongs, I am a mile-and-one-sixteenth, I am a
handicap, I am all the colors of all the silks, I am
the photo finishes, the accidents, the deaths, the
last place finishes, the breakdowns, the failure of
the toteboard, the dropped whip and the numb pain
of the dream not come true in a thousand
faces, I am the long drive home in the
dark, in the rain, I am decades and decades
of races run and won and lost and run again and I am
myself sitting with a program and a Racing Form.
I am the racetrack, my ribs are the wooden rails, my
eyes are the flashes of the toteboard, my feet are
hooves and there is something riding on my back, I am
the last turn, I am the home stretch, I am the longshot
and the favorite, I am the exacta, the daily double and
the pick-6.
I am humanly destroyed, I am the horseplayer who
became the
race and the
track.

the kid from Santiago

they brought this kid up from Chile,
expressionless, flattened
nose, shoulder blades
like angel's wings, they threw him right into
a ten-round main event against
Sugar Boy Matson
winner of 14 straight, eleven of them by
k.o., the kid's name was
Yaro, he
knocked out Matson in 2, lucky
punch maybe, so they bring in the
4th-ranked welterweight
5 weeks later and
Yaro gets him
in the 4th.
the kid gets his
hair styled, a
new Thunderbird, a blonde with
lavender eyes and
a book on English grammar.
he begins to
sniff coke and snow, gets
the 2nd-ranked welter in
the 3rd, flies
his mother up from Santiago, marries
lavender eyes,
gets the
champ, gets k.o.'d by the champ in
the 12th round. then he
goes against the
7th-ranked welter, loses
a split decision, goes against the
8th-ranked, gets a bad cut
over the right
eye and they

stop the fight; next he goes against a
new kid from Panama, gets k.o.'d in the
2nd, goes back to
Chile with his mother and
lavender eyes—
there is
money, they have been careful, they buy
a nice house, they all
sit still and look
around, he is in training
again, looks
fine, won his last 3 down
there: one
split decision, one unanimous decision,
and the last a
k.o., all against
lavender
eyes—one on the
veranda, one in the
bedroom and
the last in the backyard in the rain.
he always had fast
hands, but as they used to say,
he had to
get off fast—
get out in front—to
win. that was the
chink in his armor.
it's common, there are
lots of
men like that, and
horses
too.

room service

she comes in with all good
intentions while
I'm at
this machine.

perhaps the
sound of it
encourages her
to try to bring me more
luck and success.

but when she
enters suddenly
and I hear her
voice

I leap wildly
from this chair

scream:
"HOLY JESUS CHRIST!"

she hands me
a snack
upon a plate.

"thank you," I
tell her, "but you
really scared the
shit out of
me. you know,
when I'm at this
typer
I'm gone
around

some corner."

"sorry, daddy,"
she says, "I
forgot."

"it's all right,"
I tell her ...

only to have her
repeat
this process
the night
after next.

love, of course,
excuses
everything

and that's when
fools such as I
pick at snacks
change ribbons
clean the ashtray
and wonder
where
the last sentence
went.

passport

I went to get a passport photo.
the lady was in her late thirties
her breasts about to fall out
of her dress.
she took me in the back
and sat me down under the lights.
"you've got an interesting face,"
she said.
I wanted to tell her about her breasts
that they were interesting
but I didn't.
"are you a writer?" she asked, looking
at my paperwork.
"yes," I admitted.
she took the first shot.
"why don't you bring around some of
your books?" she asked.
"I never display my wares," I answered.
she took a second shot.
"what do you write about most?" she asked.
"women," I admitted.
"that'll be twenty dollars," she said.
I paid her.
"the photos will be ready in 3 days," she
said, "but I wish you'd bring your books
around."

I walked back down Western Ave.
crossed the bridge
over the freeway.
the retaining fence wasn't very high.
a person could quite easily fall over into the
traffic below. I walked quite a distance from
that fence.

I wanted to get safely to Paris.
I had taken a lot of abuse for that
passport photo.

darlings of the word

2 poets from San Francisco (one
quite famous) are down here in L.A.
and she's gone out to hear them
read.

I'm glad
at the moment
that
I don't have to
read in public
anymore.

I never typed this
stuff
to get up and
read it to
the mob.

I used to read for the
$$$
it helped pay the rent
but when I hear of the
famous and the well-off
still doing it
I marvel
at their
choice.

it has always seemed
curious to me
that
poets
are such
extroverts.

they love to
get up there and
warble.

I once asked a
poet about this
itch
and he told me:
"it's as old as language
itself: poets throughout
the ages
used to walk up and
down the streets
singing their rhymes,
their songs. poetry
belongs to the people."

"I don't know about that,"
I said, "but I guess even
writing for the printed
page is a form of
vanity."

"poetry belongs to the
people!" he
repeated.

"all right," I said, "let's
forget it."

if I had wanted to be
an actor
I would have gone
to Hollywood.

the only necessary
poetic act
is the writing
of the poem

and all that follows
is
propaganda.

the
teachers
the
lectures
the
readings never

can equal or
replace
what begins
it all.

2 poets from San
Francisco are
down here
now

so
far
down
here

now.

KFAC

here I sit
again
as the radio announcer
says, "for the next
3 hours we will be listening
to a selection of..."

it's now eleven p.m.
I've listened to this man's
voice
for many many years.
he must be getting quite
old.
his station plays the best
classical
music.

I don't recall how many
women I have lived with
while listening to that
announcer,
or
how many cars I've
owned
or how many places I've
lived in.

now each time I hear his
voice I think, well, he's still
alive, he sounds good
but the poor fellow must be
getting very old.

some day
he'll have his funeral,

a little trail of cars
following
the hearse.

and then
there'll be
a new voice
to listen to.

he must be very old now,
that fellow,
and every time I hear his voice
again
I pour a tall one
to salute him
happy that he's made it
for one more
night
along with me.

it is good to know
when you are done

most things work out in the end.
you walk around lighting cigarettes,
getting old, and fat, and feeling quite
common. it is only a gesture when you
put on your shoes, make love, remember, say,
once reading a novel. you even lie to your
friends about the weather and your health.
is it Wednesday or is it Thursday? you go to
a piano recital or see a football game: it's just
a way of continuing. you sleep. sleep
is best. a little nightly game of death between
you and life. you get ready. sometimes
flowers open, sometimes flowers die. you
get intoxicated. you smoke too much.
you cut your toenails. you phone somebody
who doesn't interest you. then you say,
quietly, to hell with it. *I am done.*
everybody is done, finally. it is
good to know when you are done. now you
can be a fat snake crawling into
a dark waterwell, down into the dark.
now you can know why you are alcoholic.
there are just too many sober people.
sober people are not really sober
just because they think they are. idiots
aren't sober because they do things in
their own way and disregard the world.
you don't ask for an end but it comes.
like an army drawn on funny white paper.
and it is like having wisdom in your
fingertips. it is like knowing
the names of the planets and it is like
seeing green moss on the dark side of a
tree and letting it envelop you.

the headstrong are the worst.
the headstrong become preachers then politicians
then saints and lovers. they are doomed.
the truth is in seeing straight on down the line.
there have been many good men who are now
dead, and there are yet some good living ones:
their dumb lips move and their eyes are open
and they are mute, like trees and distant stars.
it makes me sad to know
that one day they too will all be dead for
the dead are everywhere,
their armies haunt my restless nights
and yet, after all, it is so much better
that they once were here.

TB

I had it for a year, really put in
a lot of
bedroom time, slept upright on
two pillows to keep from coughing,
all the blood drained from my head
and often I'd awaken to find myself
slipping sideways off the
bed.
since my TB was contagious I didn't
have any visitors and the phone
stopped ringing
and that was the lucky
part.

during the day I tried TV and food,
neither of which went down very
well.
the soap operas and the talk shows
were a
daytime nightmare,
so for the lack of anything else
to do
I watched the baseball
games
and led the Dodgers to a
pennant.
not much else for me to do
except take antibiotics and the cough
medicine.
I also really saved putting
mileage on the car
and missed the hell out of
the old race
track.

you realize when you're
plucked out of the mainstream that
it doesn't need you or
anybody else.
the birds don't notice you're gone,
the flowers don't care,
the people out there don't notice,
but the IRS,
the phone co.,
the gas and electric co.,
the DMV, etc.,
they keep in touch.

being very sick and being dead are
very much the same
in society's
eye.

either way,
you might just as well
lay back and
enjoy it.

304

a song with no end

when Whitman wrote, "I sing the body electric"

I know what he
meant
I know what he
wanted:

to be completely alive every moment
in spite of the inevitable.

we can't cheat death but we can make it
work so hard
that when it does take
us

it will have known a victory just as
perfect as
ours.

the lucky ones

stuck in the rain on the freeway, 6:15 p.m.,
these are the lucky ones, these are the
dutifully employed, most with their radios on as loud
as possible as they try not to think or remember.

this is our new civilization: as men
once lived in trees and caves now they live
in their automobiles and on freeways as

the local news is heard again and again while
we shift from first gear to second and back to first.

there's a poor fellow stalled in the fast lane ahead, hood
up, he's standing against the freeway fence
a newspaper over his head in the rain.

the other cars force their way around his car, pull out into
the next lane in front of cars determined to shut them off.

in the lane to my right a driver is being followed by a
police car with blinking red and blue lights—he surely
can't be *speeding* as

suddenly the rain comes down in a giant wash and all the
cars stop and

even with the windows up I can smell somebody's clutch
burning.

I just hope it's not mine as

the wall of water diminishes and we go back into first
gear; we are all still
a long way from home as I memorize
the silhouette of the car in front of me and the shape of the

driver's head or
what
I can see of it above the headrest while
his bumper sticker asks me
HAVE YOU HUGGED YOUR KID TODAY?

suddenly I have the urge to scream
as another wall of water comes down and the
man on the radio announces that there will be a 70 percent
chance of showers tomorrow night.

spelling it out on my computer

enter, it says here.
delete, it says there.
return, it says.
shift, it says.
it says, control.
it says, tab.
it says, clear.
as the trees swing in the wind past midnight,
I was once twenty-five years old
and much stronger, much braver
than I am now
known halfway around the
world.

crazy as a fox

Xmas season.
I was a young boy and there was my mother and there we
were in a department store.
my mother stopped before a glass case
and I stopped too.
the case was full of toy soldiers, some with rifles
and bayonets, others were mounted on fine horses,
there were toy cannons and there were soldiers with
machine guns.
there were even realistic trenches with barbed wire
and there were airplanes and tanks.
my mother asked, "do you want some of these toy
soldiers, Henry?"
"no," I said.
I knew we were poor and I didn't want her to spend
the money
but I badly wanted those soldiers in their colored
uniforms, their different helmets with all
their stances: marching, charging, kneeling and firing.
there were officers and enlisted men, there were
flags, there were raised swords ...

"are you sure you don't want some
soldiers, Henry?"

"no, thank you," I said.

we walked on, went to another department where my
mother bought me stockings and underwear.
they would be wrapped in bright packages and
placed under the tree.

later I blamed myself and
that Christmas was disappointing but when the real war finally
came along, as wars will do, and I was found wanting by
the army psychiatrist, then
I was very pleased to recognize and accept my peculiar
insanity.

cats and you and me

the Egyptians loved the cat
were often entombed with it
instead of with the child
and never with the dog.

and now
here
good people with
the souls of cats
are very few

yet here and now many
fine cats
with great style
lounge about
in the alleys of
the universe.

about
our argument tonight
whatever it was
about
and
no matter
how unhappy
it made us
feel

remember that
there is a
cat
somewhere
adjusting to the
space of itself
with a calm

and delightful
ease.

in other words
magic persists with
or without us
no matter how
we may try to
destroy it

and I would
destroy the last chance for
myself

that this might always
continue.

they need what they need

out here near San Pedro we have
one of the largest airplanes
in the world
which doesn't fly
sitting next to
one of the largest ocean liners
in the world
which no longer cruises
and the people stand in long lines
on steaming summer afternoons
and pay
in order to
examine these lifeless
monuments.

show them something
useful and real
like a Cézanne or a Miró
and they'll just look at
you and
wonder.

hello, how are you?

this fear of being what they are:
dead.

at least they are not out on the street, they
are careful to stay indoors, those
pasty mad who sit alone before their TV sets,
their lives full of canned, mutilated laughter.

their ideal neighborhood
of parked cars
of little green lawns
of little homes
the little doors that open and close
as their relatives visit
throughout the holidays
the doors closing
behind the dying who die so slowly
behind the dead who are still alive
in your quiet average neighborhood
of winding streets
of agony
of confusion
of horror
of fear
of ignorance.

a dog standing behind a fence.

a man silent at the window.

one thirty-six a.m.

I laugh sometimes when I think about
say
Céline at a typewriter
or Dostoevsky...
or Hamsun...
ordinary men with feet, ears, eyes,
ordinary men with hair on their heads
sitting there typing words
while having difficulties with life
while being puzzled almost to madness.

Dostoevsky gets up
he leaves the machine to piss,
comes back
drinks a glass of milk and thinks about
the casino and
the roulette wheel.

Céline stops, gets up, walks to the
window, looks out, thinks, my last patient
died today, I won't have to make any more
visits there.
when I saw him last
he paid his doctor bill;
it's those who don't pay their bills,
they live on and on.
Céline walks back, sits down at the
machine
is still for a good two minutes
then begins to type.

Hamsun stands over his machine thinking,
I wonder if they are going to believe
all these things I write?
he sits down, begins to type.

he doesn't know what a writer's block
is:
he's a prolific son-of-a-bitch
damn near as magnificent as
the sun.
he types away.

and I laugh
not out loud
but all up and down these walls, these
dirty yellow and blue walls
my white cat asleep on the
table
hiding his eyes from the
light.

he's not alone tonight
and neither am
I.

harbor freeway south

the dead dogs of nowhere bark
as you approach another
traffic accident.

3 cars
one standing on its
grill
the other 2 laying
on their sides
wheels turning slowly.

3 of them
at rest:
strange angles
in the dark.

it has just
happened.

I can see the still
bodies
inside.

these cars
scattered like toys
against the freeway
center
divider.

like spacecraft
they have landed
there

as you
drive past.

there's no
ambulance yet
no police
cars.

the rain began
15 minutes
ago.

things occur.

volcanoes are
1500 times more
powerful than
the first a-
bomb.

the dead dogs of
nowhere
those dogs keep
barking.

those cars
there like that.

obscene.
a dirty trick.

it's like
somebody dying
of a heart
attack
in a crowded
elevator

everybody
watching.

I finally
reach my street
pull into

the driveway.

park.
get out.

she meets me
halfway
to the door.

"I don't know
what to do,"
she says, "the
stove
went out."

gamblers all

sometimes you climb out of bed in the morning and you think,
I'm not going to make it, but you laugh inside
remembering all the times you've felt that way, and
you walk to the bathroom, do your toilet, see that face
in the mirror, oh my oh my oh my, but you comb your hair
     anyway,
get into your street clothes, feed the cats, fetch the
newspaper of horror, place it on the coffee table, kiss your
wife goodbye, and then you are backing the car out into life itself,
like millions of others you enter the arena once more.

you are on the freeway threading through traffic now,
moving both towards something and towards nothing at all as you
     punch
the radio on and get Mozart, which is something, and you will
     somehow
get through the slow days and the busy days and the dull
days and the hateful days and the rare days, all both so delightful
and so disappointing because
we are all so alike and all so different.

you find the turn-off, drive through the most dangerous
part of town, feel momentarily wonderful as Mozart works
his way into your brain and slides down along your bones and
out through your shoes.

it's been a tough fight worth fighting
as we all drive along
betting on another day.

guitars

luckily
we don't have many
visitors
but when we do
sometimes one will
notice my wife's
guitar
propped against
the wall
and then the
night
will turn to
ruin.

"oh, a guitar!"

"yes," my wife will
say.

"do you mind?"

"of course not!"
my wife will
say.

the visitor will
go get the
guitar
come back
sit down
and begin
strumming
it.

"oh, you play?"

my wife will
ask.

"a little
bit."

the visitor will
then begin to
play.

the voice
and the
guitar are
right next to
you,
almost under
your nose.

it is an
original
work,
both the
words and the
music.

we get the
best of
everything.

the visitor
finishes.

"that was
nice!" my wife
will explain.

and the visitor
will begin
right away
to play and sing
another

original.

to me it is
embarrassing,
I don't know
why.

well, first because
the singing
isn't all that
good and
second because
there is something
about a guitar
that I just don't
like.

now
there is one song
after another.
there's no stopping
the visitor,
he or she
has a very large
repertoire.

at first I grow
dizzy, then a bit
nauseous.

the music continues.
for what seems
a lifetime.

I will finally
say,
"PLEASE!
STOP!"

the visitor will
quietly put

the guitar down
on the
coffee table.

"Hank!" my wife
will say,
"what's WRONG
with you?"

"I can't stand
it," I will
answer.

the visitor will
then be at the
door.
they will be
leaving.

"I'm sorry,"
my wife will
say.

"it's all
right," the visitor
will
respond with a
little smile.

then he or she will be
gone.

"you," my wife
will say, "you like
to hurt people's
feelings!"

"I hate guitars,"
I say, "only awful
people play
guitars."

"we've just lost
a friend!"

"so?" I
say
and walk
gratefully
up the
stairs.

no man is an island

I use valet parking at the track, it's only
3 bucks more than preferred parking.
I'm usually late and I
can leave the machine there at the entrance:
one needs only a reasonable and thoughtful
plan
to continue to pass through the
fire.

the valets see me every day and know I'm a
regular, a committed and trusted
player.
but I hold our conversations to a
minimum
my only acknowledgment of their
skill and alacrity
being the daily $2
I slip to the one who drives up in my car
as I get ready to leave
usually at the time
they are putting them in the gate
for the last
race.

now, as of late, the fellows
have been asking me
about the strange cigarettes on the car's
dash
and I inform them that
they are *eral dinesh beedies*
from India
rolled and made from the
betel leaf.

one afternoon

after having myself an excellent
$425 day
the valet who brought the car
nodded toward the
dash and asked, "hey, mind if I try
one of those?"

"not at all," I said, "and here, give some
to your buddies."
and I handed him a
pack.

then I took a few minutes to fasten my
seat belt, put on my driving
glasses, adjust the side mirror, turn
on the radio.
and when I looked before
leaving
there were the 3 or 4 valets
sitting on the long yellow
bench, each puffing on an
eral dinesh beedie.
"get high, fuckers!" I yelled
and as a group
they all waved,
laughing.

I cut right,
seeking the exit, and realized that
there are some small moments even more
important than beating the
horses.

an animal poem

I've got two kittens who are rapidly becoming
cats and at night
we share the same bed—the problem being that
they are early risers:
I am often awakened by paws and noses touching my
face.

all they do is run, eat, sleep, shit and
play
but at moments they are quiet and look
at me
with eyes
more beautiful than any human eyes I've
seen.

late at night while I rest and type
they'll hang around
say
one on the back of my chair as the other
attacks my toes.
we have a natural concern for one another, we each
need to be assured that the others are safely
there.

suddenly they'll
spring into action
run across the floor
run through the typed sheets laying there
leaving wrinkles and tiny punctures in the
poems.

then
they'll leap into the open carton of unanswered mail I've
received from my readers
and scratch furiously:

fortunately they (the cats) are house-
broken.

I expect now to write any number of cat poems
because of them
of which this is the
first.

"my god," some will say, "all Chinaski writes about
are cats!"

"my god," some used to say, "all Chinaski writes about
are whores!"

but these complainers will still keep buying my
books: they love the way I irritate
them.

this is the last poem
tonight, there's
one glass of wine left
and both of the cats
are asleep on my feet.
I can feel the gentle weight of them
the touch of their fur
I am aware of their breathing:
good things do happen and I know that as
armies everywhere march out to make
war
the kittens
at my feet
know more,
are
more,
and mean far
more
than that,
and that moments like this
can never be
forgotten.

eulogy

with old cars, especially when you buy them second-
hand and drive them for many years
a love affair is inevitable:
you even learn to
accept their little
eccentricities:
the leaking water pump
the failing plugs
the rusted throttle arm
the reluctant carburetor
the oily engine
the dead clock
the frozen speedometer and
other sundry
defects.
you also learn all the tricks to
keep the love affair alive:
how to slam the glove compartment so that
it will stay closed,
how to slap the headlight with an open palm
in order to have
light,
how many times to pump the gas pedal
and how long to wait before
touching the starter,
and you overlook each burn hole in the
upholstery
and each spring
poking through the fabric.
your car has been in and out of
police impounds,
has been ticketed for various
malfunctions:
broken wipers,
no turn signals, missing
brake light, broken tail lights, bad

brakes, excessive
exhaust and so forth
but in spite of everything
you knew you were in good hands,
there was never an accident, the
old car moved you from one place to
another,
faithfully
—the poor man's miracle.
so when that last breakdown did occur,
when the valves quit,
when the tired pistons
cracked, or the
crankshaft failed and
you sold it for
junk
—you then had to watch it carted
away
hanging there
from the back of the tow truck
wheeled off
as if it had no
soul,
the bald rear tires
the cracked back window and
the twisted license plate
were the last things you
saw, and it
hurt
as if some woman you loved very
much
and lived with
year after year
had died
and now you
would never
again know
her music
her magic
her unbelievable
fidelity.

two writers

been bothered with skin
cancer lately,
been going to the doctor
who burns the stuff
off.

strange waiting room
full of thick glossy
magazines all
about
Art.
you know, painting,
sculpture, and
etc.

about my 3rd or 4th
trip
he found out I was a
writer.

and he was working on
a Doctorate in the Arts
or some such
thing
and he laid this
massive *treatise*
on me.

"read it, read it,
let me know what you
think."

"look, doc, you
don't understand,
I write real

SIMPLE
stuff."

"that's all
right, read it,
read it ..."

so I took it
home,
375 pages,
single spaced.

something about how
when one civilization
takes over another
civilization
they leave their own
art imprinted on
it:
buildings, statues,
shrines and the
like.

that was interesting
to an
extent.
he had done his
research, plus much
personal
travel.

but
it wasn't exactly my kind
of thing.

and that's what I
told him when
I brought the
papers back.

"but what did you

think of it?"

"good, yeah, good."

"what's that on your
ear?"

"I dunno ..."

"come on in and I'll
burn it off."

he did that.
I smelled burning
flesh.
it seemed to take a long
time.
then he was
finished.

"when are you going
to give me one of
your books?" he
asked.

"next time."

I walked out and
had the girl
charge it to
Medicare.

"he's writing better
all the time,"
she said.

"so am I," I
said.

then I walked out
of there

to my car
in the parking lot,
trying to stay out
of the
sun.

small conversation in the afternoon
with John Fante

he said, "I was working in Hollywood when Faulkner was
working in Hollywood and he was
the worst: he was too drunk to stand up at the
end of the afternoon and so I had to help him
into a taxi
day after day after day.

"but when he left Hollywood, I stayed on, and while I
didn't drink like that maybe I should have, I might have
had the guts then to follow him and get the hell out of
there."

I told him, "you write as well as
Faulkner."

"you mean that?" he asked from the hospital
bed, smiling.

girl on the escalator

as I go to the escalator
a young fellow and a lovely young girl
are ahead of me.
her pants, her blouse are skin-
tight.
as we ascend
she rests one foot on the
step above and her behind
assumes a fascinating shape.
the young man looks all
around.
he appears worried.
he looks at me.
I look
away.

no, young man, I am not looking,
I am *not* looking at your girl's behind.
don't worry, I respect her and I respect you.
in fact, I respect everything: the flowers that grow, young women,
children, all the animals, our precious complicated
universe, everyone and everything.

I sense that the young man now feels
better and I am glad for
him. I know his problem: the girl has
a mother, a father, maybe a sister or
brother, and undoubtedly a bunch of
unfriendly relatives and she likes to
dance and flirt and she likes to
go to the movies and sometimes she talks
and chews gum at the same time and
she enjoys really dumb TV shows and
she thinks she's a budding actress and she
doesn't always look so good and she has a

336

terrible temper and sometimes she almost goes
crazy and she can talk for hours on the
telephone and she wants to go to
Europe some summer soon and she wants you to
buy her a near-new Mercedes and she's in love with
Mel Gibson and her mother is a
drunk and her father is a racist
and sometimes when she drinks too much she
snores and she's often cold in bed and
she has a guru, a guy who met Christ
in the desert in 1978, and she wants to
be a dancer and she's unemployed and she
gets migraine headaches every time she
eats sugar or cheese.

I watch him take her
up
the escalator, his arm
protectively about her
waist, thinking he's
lucky,
thinking he's a real special
guy, thinking that
nobody in the world has
what he has.

and he's right, terribly
terribly right, his arm around
that warm bucket of
intestine,
bladder,
kidneys,
lungs,
salt,
sulphur,
carbon dioxide
and
phlegm.

lotsa
luck

one learns

one learns to endure because not to endure
turns the world over to them
and they are less than
zero.

to endure means to simply gut-it-out
and the worse the odds
the more enjoyable the
victory.

they say you must fight for your
freedom.
I know that.
only I didn't fight the Japanese, the Italians, the Germans
or the Russians
for my freedom.
I fought Americans: the parents, the school yards,
the bosses, the ladies of the street, the friends, the
system
itself.

there's no end, of course, to the fight.
new difficulties arrive like a train on time.
it may no longer be the hangover morning or the
factory assembly line
but treachery, deceit, and false hope take their
place.
I believe we are tested even as we
sleep, and often it all gets so deadly
we can only laugh it away.

to endure takes some luck, some knowledge and a
reasonable sense of
humor because the cold have gotten colder,
the strong stronger,

the once-bold less-bold and
all that's left for us is
to consider the way
the elephant stands silent in the forest waiting to die,
the way men fail again and again and again,
the way the priest forgets his prayers,
the way love can turn to folly,
or the way the cold rain soaks Mozart's
grave. it's in spite of these and
so many other things that
one learns finally how to
endure.

the beginning of a brief love affair

a poem with a head like a duck
and camel's feet
belly of the whale
snake eyes
arrow in its bellybutton
spider fingers
rabbit skin
frosted like an iceberg
with an ugly smile
and shining white teeth
sits in this machine
and grins up at me
as a young man slams the lid
on the trash bin outside.
I like this poem
as it looks up at me and
I don't always like the poems
as they look up at me
from this machine.
so, goodbye young man,
get rid of your trash
go on up the street
hang around the taco stand
try an adult bookstore
seize your liberty
the world may be yours but
I'm not finished yet.

melodies that echo

thinking back to the time when
I was starving to death trying to become
a writer (which was a long time ago)
I can still remember some of the popular songs
of the day:
"a tisket, a tasket, a little yellow
basket"
"I can't give you anything but love,
baby"
"when the deep purple falls over sleepy
garden walls"
"the man I love"
"anything goes"
"body and soul"
"I get a kick out of
you!"

melodies that echo
through the long halls of memory
as you
wonder again how Faulkner ever did
it down in Mississippi,
or Ezra
after they pulled him in a cage
through the streets of
Italy,
or T. S. Eliot as he counted change in his
teller's cage,
or Lorca before he was shot down like a dog
in the road.

"my heart belongs to Daddy"
"by the light of the silvery moon"
"let's do it!"
"them there eyes"

"it's d'lovely"
and
"you are my shining
star."

self-inflicted wounds

he talked about Steinbeck and Thomas Wolfe and he
wrote like a cross between the two of them
and I lived in a hotel on Figueroa Street
close to the bars
and he lived further uptown in a small room
and we both wanted to be writers
and we'd meet at the public library, sit on the stone
benches and talk about that.
he showed me his short stories and he wrote well, he
wrote better than I did, there was a calm and a
strength in his work that mine did not have.
my stories were jagged, harsh, with self-inflicted wounds.

I showed him all my work but he was more impressed with
my drinking prowess and my worldly attitude

after talking a bit we would go to Clifton's Cafeteria
for our only meal of the day
(for less than a dollar in 1941)
yet
we were in great health.
we lost jobs, found jobs, lost jobs.
mostly we didn't work, we always envisioned we soon
would be receiving regular checks from
The New Yorker, The Atlantic Monthly and
Harper's.

we ran with a gang of young men who didn't envision
anything at all
but they had a gallant lawless charm
and we drank with them and fought with them and
had a hell of a wild good time.

then just like that he joined the Marine Corps.
"I want to prove something to myself" was what he told

me.

he did: right after boot camp the war came and in 3 months
he was dead.
and I promised myself that some day I would write a novel and
    that
I would dedicate it to him.

I have now written 5 novels, all dedicated to others.

you know, you were right, Robert Baun, when you once told
me, "Bukowski, about half of what you say is
bullshit."

racetrack parking lot
at the end of the day

I watch them push the crippled and the infirm
in their wheelchairs
on to the electric lift
which carries them up into the long bus
where each chair is locked down
and each person has a window
of their own.
they are all white-skinned, like
pale paint on thin cardboard;
most of them are truly old;
there are a number of women, a few old
men, and 3 surprisingly young men
2 of whom wear neck braces that *gleam*
in the late afternoon sun
and all 3 with arms as thin as
rope and hands that resemble clenched
claws.
the caretaker seems very kind, very
understanding, he's a
marvelous fat fellow with a
rectangular head and he wears a broad
smile which is not
false.
the old women are either extremely thin
or overweight.
most have humped backs and shoulders
and wispy
very straight
white hair.
they sit motionless, look straight
ahead as the electric lift raises them
on to the bus.
there is no conversation;
they appear calm and not embittered

by their plight. both men and women
are soon loaded on to the waiting bus except for
the last one, a very old man, almost skeletal,
with a tiny round head, completely bald, a
shining white dot against the late afternoon sky,
waving a cane above his head as he is
pushed shouting on to the electric lift:
"WELL, THEY ROBBED OUR ASSES
AGAIN, CLEANED US OUT, WE'RE A
BUNCH OF SUCKERS TOTTERING ON THE
EDGE OF OUR GRAVES AND WE LET THEM TAKE
OUR LAST PENNY AGAIN!"
as he speaks
he waves the cane above his head and
cracks the marvelous fat fellow
who is pushing his chair,
cracks the cane against the side of
the caretaker's head.
it's a mighty blow and
the attendant staggers, grabs
hard at the back of the
wheelchair
as the old man yells: "OH, JERRY,
I'M SORRY, I'M SO SORRY, WHAT CAN I
DO? WHAT
CAN I DO?"

Jerry steadies himself, he is not badly hurt.
it's a small concussion but within an hour
he will possess a knot the size of an
apricot.

"it's all right, Sandy, only
I've told you again and again, please
be careful with that damned
cane ..."

Sandy is pushed on to the electric
lift, it rises and he disappears into
the bus's dark interior.

then Jerry climbs slowly into the bus, takes
the wheel, starts up, the door closes with a hiss,
the bus begins to move to the exit,
and on the back of the vehicle
in bold white letters
on dark blue background
I see the words:
HARBOR HOME OF LOVE.

moving toward what?

river down, grapes pressed
summer is over
again
and the lovers
of
most things can
no longer find anything to
love.

my 5 proud cats lie
about the house
listening to the hard cold
rain

even as autumn is now gone
again

as Xmas and New
Years
those twin plagues
wait patiently again
for me.

my wife now
asleep in the bedroom
upstairs
her small child's
body
yearning for the
good
dream.

river down, grapes pressed
this time is
the

sad
great
blade

please please
please
let the inevitable
become

finally as
meaningful
and as
beautiful

as
my
5 proud cats
now sleeping and
no longer listening
to
the hard cold
rain.

if I had failed to make the struggle

there would be no peace, no solace, no
wisdom.
night would follow night
like a string of ants
come to carry you
off.
in a world cluttered with the falsely
famous
there would be no
escape.
you would face a hard
impossibility while
chewing on your toast
or cleaning your
teeth
or waiting for the
result
of a photo finish
or a cancer
checkup.

there would be no voice to
listen to,
no acceptable
god.
even the laughter you once
enjoyed, they would have
stripped even that from
you
and left you
to be worn down
finally
like water upon
stone.

in the beginning youth
fought them
off;
middle age was there to contemplate the
wounds;
and now
maturity
is here to record
a simple
victory.

wine pulse

this is another poem about 2 a.m. and how I'm still at the
machine listening to the radio and smoking a good
cigar.
hell, I don't know, sometimes I feel just like Van Gogh or
    Faulkner or,
say, Stravinsky, as I sip wine and type
and smoke and there's no magic as gentle as this.
some critics say I write the same things over and over.
well, sometimes I do and sometimes I don't, but when I do the
reason is that it feels so right, it's like making love and
if you knew how good it felt you would forgive me
because we both know how fickle happiness can be.
so I play the fool and say again that
it's 2 a.m.
and that I am
Cézanne
Chopin
Céline
Chinaski
embracing everything:
the sweep of cigar smoke
another glass of wine
the beautiful young girls
the criminals and the killers
the lonely mad
the factory workers,
this machine here,
the radio playing,
I repeat it all again
and I'll repeat it all forever
until the magic that happens to me
happens to you.

PHOTO: Michael Montfort

CHARLES BUKOWSKI is one of America's best-known contemporary writers of poetry and prose, and, many would claim, its most influential and imitated poet. He was born in Andernach, Germany, to an American soldier father and a German mother in 1920, and brought to the United States at the age of three. He was raised in Los Angeles and lived there for fifty years. He published his first story in 1944 when he was twenty-four and began writing poetry at the age of thirty-five. He died in San Pedro, California, on March 9, 1994, at the age of seventy-three, shortly after completing his last novel, *Pulp* (1994).

During his lifetime he published more than forty-five books of poetry and prose, including the novels *Post Office* (1971), *Factotum* (1975), *Women* (1978), *Ham on Rye* (1982), and *Hollywood* (1989). Among his most recent books are the posthumous editions of *What Matters Most Is How Well You Walk Through the Fire* (1999), *Open All Night: New Poems* (2000), *Beerspit Night and Cursing: The Correspondence of Charles Bukowski and Sheri Martinelli* (2001), and *Night Torn Mad with Footsteps: New Poems* (2001).

All of his books have now been published in translation in more than a dozen languages and his worldwide popularity remains undiminished. In the years to come Ecco will publish additional volumes of previously uncollected poetry and letters.